THE
EASTERN
EUROPE
COLLECTION

COMENIUS
AND THE BEGINNINGS
OF EDUCATIONAL REFORM

Will S. Monroe

ARNO PRESS & THE NEW YORK TIMES

New York - 1971

Reprint Edition 1971 by Arno Press Inc.

LC# 78-135824

ISBN 0-405-02765-6

The Eastern Europe Collection
ISBN for complete set: 0-405-02730-3

Manufactured in the United States of America

COMENIUS

The Great Educators

EDITED BY NICHOLAS MURRAY BUTLER

COMENIUS

AND

THE BEGINNINGS OF EDUCATIONAL REFORM

BY

WILL S. MONROE, A.B.

PROFESSOR OF PSYCHOLOGY AND PEDAGOGY IN THE
STATE NORMAL SCHOOL AT WESTFIELD, MASS.

NEW YORK

CHARLES SCRIBNER'S SONS

1900

Norwood Press
J. S. Cushing & Co. — Berwick & Smith
Norwood Mass. U.S.A.

PREFACE

THE present volume is an effort to trace the reform movement in education from Vives, Bacon, and Ratke to Comenius, who gave the movement its most significant force and direction; and from him to the later reformers, — Francke, Rousseau, Basedow, Pestalozzi, Fröbel, and Herbart. A variety of ideas, interests, and adaptations, all distinctly modern, are represented in the life-creeds of these reformers; and, in the absence of a more satisfactory term, the progressive movement which they represent has been styled realism, — sometimes called the "new education."

It has been well said that "the dead hand of spiritual ancestry lays no more sacred duty on posterity than that of realizing under happier circumstances ideas which the stress of age or the shortness of life has deprived of their accomplishment." Many of the reforms represented by the realists occupy no inconsiderable place in the platforms of modern practitioners of education; and in the belief that a history of the movement might contribute toward the ultimate reforms which realism represents, it has seemed expedient to focus such a survey on the life and teachings of the strongest personality and chief exponent of the movement.

The condition of education in Europe during the sixteenth century is briefly told in the opening chapter; following are given the traces of the educational development of Comenius in the writings of Vives, Bacon, and Ratke; three chapters are devoted to the life of Comenius and the reforms in which he actively participated; an exposition of his educational writings has three chapters; a chapter is given to the influence of Comenius on Francke, Rousseau, Pestalozzi, and other modern reformers; and the closing chapter sums up his permanent influence. The volume has two appendices, — one giving tables of dates relating to the life and writings of Comenius, and the other a select annotated bibliography.

In the exposition of the writings of Comenius, the author has made liberal use of English and German translations from Latin and Czech originals. In the case of the *Great didactic*, the scholarly translation by Mr. Keatinge has, in the main, been followed. Free translations of portions of this work had been made by the author before the appearance of Mr. Keatinge's book; and in some instances these have been retained. As regards the account of Comenius' views on the earliest education of the child, the author's edition of the *School of infancy* has been followed; and in the discussion of reforms in language teaching, he is indebted to Mr. Bardeen's edition of the *Orbis pictus*, and to Dr. William T. Harris for the use of the handsome Elzevir edition of the *Janua*, which is the property of the Bureau of Education.

WILL S. MONROE.

State Normal School,
Westfield, Mass.

CONTENTS

CHAPTER V

CLOSING YEARS: 1656-1670

CHAPTER VI

PHILOSOPHY OF EDUCATION

CHAPTER VII

EARLIEST EDUCATION OF THE CHILD

CHAPTER VIII

STUDY OF LANGUAGE

CHAPTER IX

INFLUENCE OF COMENIUS ON MODERN EDUCATORS

COMENIUS

CHAPTER I

EUROPEAN EDUCATION IN THE SIXTEENTH CENTURY

Humanism, realism, and naturalism characterized — Devotion of
the sixteenth century to the humanistic ideal — Study of Latin
eloquence — Style the chief aim — Neglect of the mother-tongue
— Views of John Sturm and the Jesuits — Devotion to Cicero —
Decadence of the later humanists — Erasmus and Melanchthon
on the enrichment of the course of study — Satires of Rabelais
directed against the humanists — Protests of Montaigne — Attitude of Ascham and Mulcaster — Transition from humanism to
realism.

"EDUCATION in Europe," says Oscar Browning,[1]
"has passed through three phases, which may conven-
iently be called humanism, realism, and naturalism.
The first is grounded upon the study of language, and
especially of the two dead languages, Greek and Latin.
The second is based upon the study of things instead
of words, the education of the mind through the eye
and the hand. Closely connected with this is the
study of those things which may be of direct influence upon and direct importance to life. The third is
not in the first instance study at all. It is an attempt

---

[1] *Aspects of education.* By Oscar Browning. New York: Industrial Educational Association, 1888.

to build up the whole nature of man,—to educate first his body, then his character, and lastly his mind."

The sixteenth century was wedded to the humanistic ideal of education. Without regard for the diversity of avocations, classical culture was held to be the safest and best training for the manifold duties of life. Aristotle's *Politics* was considered the wisest utterance on the direction of affairs of state; Cæsar's *Commentaries* the safest guides to military eminence; the practical Stoicism of the Latin authors the most infallible basis for ethics and the regulation of conduct; and as for agriculture, had not Virgil written a treatise on that subject? It was clear in the minds of the sixteenth-century humanists that classical culture furnished the best preparation, alike for theologians and artisans.

To accomplish this purpose, as soon as the child was considered sufficiently matured for linguistic discipline, and this varied from the sixth to the ninth years, he was initiated into the mysteries of Latin eloquence. His preliminary training consisted in a verbal study of the Latin grammar for purposes of precision in speech and successful imitation; but, as the grammar was printed in Latin, with its hundreds of incomprehensible rules and exceptions, all of which had to be "learned by heart," the way of the young learner was, indeed, a thorny one. True, the classical authors were later read, but chiefly for the purpose of gleaning from them choice phrases to be used in the construction of Latin sentences, or for purposes of disputations in dialectics. Logic and history were given most subordinate places in the course of study, the former merely that it might give greater precision in writing and speaking, and the latter that it might furnish illustrations in rhetorical exercises.

This conception of education was almost universally held in the sixteenth century, by Protestants like Trotzendorf and Sturm, as well as by Catholics like Aquaviva and the members of the Society of Jesus. Nor was it confined to elementary and secondary education; for, as Professor Paulsen[1] has shown, the conquest of European universities by the humanists was complete by the second decade of the sixteenth century. The statutes of most of the universities at this time make the speaking of the Latin compulsory. That at Ingolstadt reads: "A master in a bursary shall induce to the continual use of Latin by verbal exhortations and by his own example; and shall also appoint those who shall mark such as speak the vulgar tongue and shall receive from them an irremissible penalty." Again: "That the students in their academical exercises may learn by the habit of speaking Latin to speak and express themselves better, the faculty ordains that no person placed by the faculty upon a common or other bursary shall dare to speak German. Any one heard by one of the overseers to speak German shall pay one kreutzer." There grew out of this prohibition a widespread system of spying. The spies reported to the university authorities on such students (*vulgarisantes* they were called) who persisted in speaking in the mother-tongue. In spite, however, of statutes, spies, fines, and floggings, the

---

[1] *The German universities: their character and historical development.* By Friedrich Paulsen. Authorized translation by Edward Delavan Perry, with an introduction by Nicholas Murray Butler. New York and London: Macmillan & Co., 1895. pp. xxxi + 254.

boys in the sixteenth century spoke little Latin when they were alone by themselves. Cordier,[1] writing in 1530, says, "Our boys always chatter French with their companions; or if they try to talk Latin, cannot keep it up."

The old ecclesiastical Latin of the Middle Ages had been superseded by the classical Latin of the Roman poets, and all the energies of the educational institutions were thrown into the acquisition and practice of Latin eloquence. The classics were read for the phrases that might be culled for use in the construction of Latin sentences; these, with disputations, declamations, and Latin plays, were the order of the century. Since education consisted in the acquisition of a graceful and elegant style, the young learner, from the first, applied himself to the grammatical study of Latin authors, regarding solely the language of the classics, and taking subject-matter into account only when this was necessary to understand the words.

There was no study of the mother-tongue preliminary to the study of the classics. Children began at once the study of the Latin grammar, and they had to write Latin verses before they had been exercised in compositions, in the vernacular, or, for that matter, before they had been trained to express their thoughts in Latin prose. And still more remarkable, as Oscar Browning points out, "the Latin taught was not the masculine language of Lucretius and Cæsar, but the ornate and artificial diction of Horace and Virgil, and, above all, of Cicero." "There is no doubt," he adds, "that narrow and faulty as it was, it gave a good edu-

---

[1] *De corrupti sermonis emendatione.* By Maturin Cordier. Paris, 1530. Quoted by Mr. Keatinge.

cation so long as people believed in it. To know Horace and Virgil by heart became the first duty of the scholar. Speeches in Parliament were considered incomplete if they did not contain at least one Latin quotation. A false quantity was held to be a greater crime than a slip in logical argument. Cicero not only influenced the education of English statesmen, but had no inconsiderable effect on their conduct."

The humanist educators of the sixteenth century not only neglected the study of the mother-tongue — they proscribed it. The *Ratio*[1] of the Jesuits forbids its use except on holidays, and Sturm at Strasburg abbreviated the recreation periods of his pupils because of risks of speaking in the mother-tongue on the playground. And all this proscription of the vernacular that students might acquire eloquence in a foreign tongue. Well does Raumer[2] ask, "Why did they continue, like a second Sisyphus, their fruitless endeavors to metamorphose German into Roman youths, and to impart to them, in defiance of the laws of human nature, another tongue?"

They were themselves deceived in assuming that they could call to life the ancient. culture of Rome and Greece. Indeed, they believed that they had discovered ways of training which would develop scholars capable of producing Latin works equal to the masterpieces that they had studied in their schools. John Sturm, one of the most ardent of the humanists, said:

---

[1] For an account of the schools of the Jesuits see *Loyola and the educational system of the Jesuits.* By Thomas Hughes. New York: Charles Scribner's Sons, 1892. pp. 302.

[2] *Geschichte der Pädagogik.* Von Karl von Raumer. Gütersloh: Bertelsmann, 1882.

"The Romans had two advantages over us; the one consisted in learning Latin without going to school, and the other in frequently seeing Latin comedies and tragedies acted, and in hearing Latin orators speak. Could we recall these advantages in our schools, why could we not, by persevering diligence, gain what they possessed by accident and habit — namely, the power of speaking Latin to perfection? I hope to see the men of the present age, in their writing and speaking, not merely followers of the old masters, but equal to those who flourished in the noblest age of Athens and Rome." But how misguided and mistaken!

Not only did Latin monopolize the curriculum of the sixteenth-century school, but the study was primarily philological, for grammatical structure, and only secondarily for the content of the literature, for a correct understanding of the author. As a matter of fact, the method of study was such as to make intelligent comprehension of the author's thought next to impossible, since the humanists simply culled out phrases which might be imitated and used in the exercises of style. Raumer says of this kind of teaching: "The author was not an end, but only a means to an end — the cultivation of deified Roman eloquence in boys. And why? Precisely as the peacock was used by the jackdaw. They borrowed the author's words and phrases, grouped them together, and learned them by heart, in order subsequently to apply them in speech or writing. Borrow is too feeble an expression; for the jackdaw designed not merely to borrow the peacock's feathers, but to represent them as his own. The doctrine of imitation, as set forth by Sturm and the others, was, after all, a mere jackdaw theory.

The pupil was taught how, by a slight alteration, to disguise phrases from Cicero, and then to use them in writing or speech, exactly as if they were his own productions, so adroitly smuggling them in that the readers or hearers might not suspect from whence they were taken. Says Sturm: 'When the teacher gives out themes for composition, he should draw attention to those points where imitation is desirable, and show how similarity may be concealed by a superadded variation.' Again: 'We must, in the first place, take care that the similarity shall not be manifest. Its concealment may be accomplished in three ways — by adding, by taking away, and by alteration.' "

In this mad race for Latin eloquence, the sixteenth-century humanists became more and more circumscribed in the choice of authors. Sturm, for example, placed Cicero at the head of the list, because of the faultless models of his eloquence. The Jesuits likewise held Cicero in high esteem. Said one of their writers, "Style should be drawn almost exclusively from Cicero, although the most approved of the historians need not on that account be overlooked." Again: "The pattern we should follow in style is comprehended in the words of the rule, 'imitate Cicero.' As in the study of theology we follow the divine Thomas Aquinas, and in philosophy Aristotle, so in the humanities Cicero must be regarded as our peculiar and preëminent leader. For he has been crowned by the palm of superior praise by the common consent of the world. But some, misguided by a wilful and self-formed taste, have gone astray, preferring a style totally different from that of Cicero; such an erratic course is quite at variance with the genius of our institutions and hostile to the spirit of prompt obedience."

This servile devotion to Cicero, it should be recalled, was a marked departure from the more varied and richer curricula of the fifteenth-century humanists,[1] when men of the stamp of Vittorino da Feltre, Leonardo Bruni, Vergarius, Sylvius, and Guarino were the standard-bearers of humanism. Many causes had conspired to bring about this decadence; and perhaps the most fundamental cause was the senseless worship of forms of expression. The later humanists worshipped the *forms* of thought. "Beauty of expression," says Professor Laurie,[2] "was regarded as inseparable from truth and elevation of thought. The movement soon shared the fate of all enthusiasms. The new form was worshipped, and to it the spirit and substance were subordinated. Style became the supreme object of the educated classes, and successful imitation, and thereafter laborious criticism, became marks of the highest culture."

This use of the classics as instruments in grammatical drill and vehicles of communication had become well-nigh universal by the middle of the sixteenth century. Erasmus, himself one of the most ardent advocates of classical learning, perceived apparently the narrowing tendencies of humanistic training, and urged that students be taught to know many things besides Latin and Greek in order that they might the

---

[1] See the admirable sketch of the earlier humanists: *Vittorino da Feltre and other humanists*. By William H. Woodward. Cambridge: University Press, 1897. pp. 256.

[2] *John Amos Comenius: his life and educational work*. By S. S. Laurie. Boston: Willard Small, 1885. pp. 229.

better comprehend the classics. He recommended the addition of geography, arithmetic, and natural science to the school course.

And Melanchthon, with all his enthusiasm for classical learning, thought the humanities insufficient to satisfy all the needs of culture. He advised the incorporation of physics, mathematics, and astronomy into the curriculum. "Although the nature of things cannot be absolutely known, nor the marvellous works of God traced to their original, until, in the future life, we shall listen to the eternal counsel of the Father," he writes, "nevertheless, even amid this our present darkness, every gleam and every hint of harmony of this fair creation forms a step toward the knowledge of God and toward virtue, whereby we ourselves shall also learn to love and maintain order and moderation in all our acts. Since it is evident that men are endowed by their Creator with faculties fitted for the contemplation of nature, they must, of necessity, take delight in investigating the elements, the laws, the qualities, and the forces of the various bodies by which they are surrounded."

As has already been shown, however, the humanists took little interest in the study of subjects not discussed by classical authors. Absorbed in a world of books, as Mr. Quick [1] suggests, they overlooked the world of nature. Galileo had in vain tried to persuade them to look through his telescope, but they held that truth could not be discovered by any such contrivances — that it could be arrived at only by the comparison of manuscripts. "No wonder," remarks Mr. Quick,

[1] *Essays on educational reformers.* By Robert Hebert Quick. New York: D. Appleton & Co., 1893. pp. 560.

"that they had so little sympathy with children, and did not know how to teach them."

Fortunately for the history of education, there were critics in the sixteenth century who did not conform to the dogma of linguistic discipline, and who called attention to the need of educational reform. Whatever the merits of the classical languages, protested these critics, they must derive their value ultimately from the rank they take as literature. The protest of Rabelais early in the century was not only one of the first but one of the most effective charges against contemporary practices. In his famous satire he intrusted the young giant Gargantua to the care and training of the humanist educator Tubal Holofernes, who spent five years and a quarter in teaching him to say his A B C's backward; thirteen years on Donatus' Latin grammar and the composition of Latin verses and sentences; thirty-four years more in the study of Latin eloquence, after which the schoolmaster dies, when, as Rabelais concluded, Gargantua had grown more ignorant, heavy, and loutish. "In this confused and ribald allegory," says Mr. James P. Munroe,[1] "Rabelais led the way out of ancient superstition into modern science. More than this, he taught in it that the study of Nature, observation of her laws, imitation of her methods, must be at the root of every true system of education. He showed that the Nature spirit is the true spirit of good teaching. Ever since his day civilized mankind has been trying to learn this lesson of his and to apply it in the schools. For three centuries

[1] *The educational ideal: an outline of its growth in modern times.* By James Phinny Munroe. Boston: D. C. Heath & Co., 1895. pp. 262.

the leaders in education, under his direct inspiration, have been slowly and painfully transforming the false pedagogy of the cloister into the true pedagogy of out-of-doors. Writers and teachers, schools and universities, have been engaged in a halting and irregular struggle to transfer education from a metaphysical to a physical basis, to lead it away from the habit of deductive speculation into one of inductive research. This transfer Rabelais made boldly and at once. He did not, of course, elaborate the educational ideal of to-day, but he plainly marked out the lines upon which that ideal is framed. He taught truth and simplicity, he ridiculed hypocrisy and formalism, he denounced the worship of words, he demanded the study of things, he showed the beauty of intellectual health, of moral discipline, of real piety. Best of all, he enunciated the supreme principle of Nature, which is *ordered freedom.*"

Montaigne,[1] also, in France, was equally severe in his criticisms on the humanists. He denounced in no uncertain terms the methods of introducing Latin to beginners and the harsh and severe discipline so common in the schools of Europe during the sixteenth century. "Education ought to be carried on with a severe sweetness," he wrote, "quite contrary to the practice of our pedants, who, instead of tempting and alluring children to a study of language by apt and gentle ways, do, in truth, present nothing before them but rods and ferules, horror and cruelty. Away with this violence! Away with this compulsion! There is nothing which more completely dulls and degenerates

---

[1] *Montaigne's Education of children.* Translated by L. E. Rector. New York: D. Appleton & Co., 1899. pp. xxiii + 191.

the nature of a bright child." Again: "Our schools
are houses of correction for imprisoned youths; and
children are made incorrigible by punishment. Visit
them when the children are getting their lessons, and
you will hear nothing but the outcries of boys under
execution and the thundering noises of their teachers,
drunk with fury. It is a pernicious way to tempt
young and timorous souls to love their books while
wearing a ferocious countenance and with a rod in
hand."

Montaigne was equally convinced of the pedagogic
error of the humanists in regarding classical knowledge
as synonymous with wisdom. "We may become
learned from the learning of others," he said, "but we
never become wise except by our own wisdom. . . .
We are truly learned from knowing the present, not
from knowing the past any more than the future. . . .
Yet we toil only to stuff the memory and leave the
conscience and understanding void. And like birds
abroad to forage for grain, bring it home in their beak,
without tasting it themselves, to feed their young, so
our pedants go picking knowledge here and there out
of several authors, and hold it at their tongue's end,
only to spit it out and distribute it among their pupils."

Roger Ascham,[1] in the quaint preface of his *Scholemaster*, also bears testimony against the harsh discipline of the sixteenth century. During the great
plague in London, in 1563, Ascham and some friends
were dining at Windsor with Sir William Cecil.
While there he learned that many of the students at
Eton had run away because of the severe punishments

[1] *The scholemaster.* By Roger Ascham. Edited by Edward
Arber. Boston; Willard Small, 1888. pp. 317.

administered at this famous public school. "Whereupon," says Ascham, "Sir William took occasion to
wish that some discretion were in many schoolmasters
in using correction than commonly there is, who
many times punish rather the weakness of nature than
the fault of the scholar, whereby many scholars that
might else prove well, be driven to hate learning
before they know what learning meaneth; and so are
made willing to forsake their book, and to be willing
to put to any other kind of living." This incident led
to the composition of the *Scholemaster*, which was a
guide for "the bringing up of youth," in which gentle-
ness rather than severity is recommended, and "a
ready way to the Latin tongue," in which an honest
effort is made to simplify language teaching and adapt
it to the tastes and interests of young learners.

Richard Mulcaster,[1] another Englishman and humanist of the sixteenth century, questioned seriously the
wisdom of his associates and contemporaries in
their exclusion of the mother-tongue from the course
of study. In his *Elementarie* he asked: "Is it not
a marvellous bondage to become servants to one
tongue, for learning's sake, the most part of our time,
with loss of most time, whereas we may have the very
same treasure in our own tongue with the gain of most
time? our own bearing the joyful title of our liberty
and freedom, the Latin tongue remembering us of our
thraldom and bondage. I love Rome, but London
better; I favor Italy, but England more: I honor the
Latin, but I worship the English." Mr. Quick is
right in maintaining that "it would have been a vast

[1] *Positions*. By Richard Mulcaster. Edited by Robert Hebert
Quick. London: Longmans, Green & Co., 1888. pp. 309.

gain to all Europe if Mulcaster had been followed instead of Sturm. He was one of the earliest advocates of the use of English instead of Latin, and good reading and writing in English were to be secured before Latin was begun."

These were some of the voices raised against the bookish classical learning of the sixteenth century; but it remained for Vives, Bacon, and Ratke to convince Europe of the insufficiency of the humanistic ideal, and for Comenius, the evangelist of modern pedagogy, to bring about the necessary reforms. The part played by each in the transition from humanism to realism, from classical learning and philology to modern thought and the natural sciences, will be briefly traced in the succeeding chapters of this work.

CHAPTER II

FORERUNNERS OF COMENIUS

Traces of the intellectual development of Comenius. Vives a realist — His early training in Spain and France — Educational activity in Belgium and England — Views on the education of women
— Theory of education — Comparison of Vives and Comenius.
Bacon the founder of modern realism — Views on the education
of his day — Attacks mediævalism — Study of nature and the
inductive method — Individual differences among children.
Ratke — Studies at Hamburg and Rostock — Visits England and
becomes acquainted with the philosophy of Bacon — His plan of
education — Its reception by the universities at Jena and Giessen
— Organization of the schools at Gotha — Call to Sweden — Summary of Ratke's views — Harmony of his teachings with those
of Comenius. Campanella, Andreæ, and Bateus — Their influence on the life and teachings of Comenius.

EVERY educational reformer owes much, in the way
of inspiration and suggestion, to his predecessors, and
of none is this more true than of John Amos Comenius.
Everywhere in his writings are to be found traces of
the movement he championed, in the writings of
Vives, Bacon, Ratke, Bateus, Campanella, and others.
As Professor Nicholas Murray Butler remarks: "From
Ratke he learned something of the way in which
language teaching, the whole curriculum of the time,
might be reformed; and from Bateus he derived both
the title and the plan of his *Janua*. Campanella suggested to him the necessity of the direct interrogation
of nature if knowledge was to progress, and Vives
emphasized for him from the same point of view the

defects of contemporary school practice. But it was Bacon's *Instauratio Magna* that opened his eyes to the possibilities of our knowledge of nature and its place in the educational scheme."[1] This obligation to his predecessors Comenius was the first to recognize. And he recognized it often and specifically by his willing tributes to the help received by him from Vives, Bacon, Ratke, and others.

Vives

"Comenius received his first impulse as a sense-realist," says Raumer, "from the well-known Spanish pedagogue John Lewis Vives, who had come out against Aristotle and disputation in favor of a Christian mode of philosophizing and the silent contemplation of nature." "It is better for the pupils to ask, to investigate, than to be forever disputing with one another," said Vives. "Yet," adds Comenius, "Vives understood better where the fault was than what was the remedy." In the preface to the *Janua*, Comenius quotes Vives among others as opposed to the current methods of language teaching.

The Spanish educator was born a hundred years before Comenius, of poor, but noble parentage. When fifteen years old he was considered the most brilliant pupil in the academy at Valencia. Two years later he was matriculated in the University of Paris, where, as his biographers tell us, he was surrounded by the Dialecticians, whose theology was the most abstruse and whose Latin was the most barbarous. This con-

[1] *The place of Comenius in the history of education.* By Nicholas Murray Butler. Proceedings of the National Educational Association for 1892.

dition of affairs turned the young Spaniard's thoughts toward educational reform. He realized in Paris, as he had not before, the uselessness of the empty disputations which occupied so much time in the schools.

Three years were spent in study at Paris, after which Vives travelled through portions of Spain and France, and, in 1517, he settled with the Valdura family in Bruges and married the daughter of his host. Here he wrote his allegory *Christi triumphus*, in which he holds up to ridicule the methods of teaching in the University of Paris. A year later he was installed in the University of Louvain as the instructor of the young Cardinal de Croy. While here he wrote a history of philosophy; made the acquaintance of Erasmus; and opened correspondence with Thomas More and other reformers.

In 1519 he visited Paris with Cardinal de Croy; and, in spite of his late criticisms, he was cordially received by the university, his scholarship and ability now being recorded facts. Two years later De Croy died without having made any provision for the support of his tutor. Vives began at once a commentary on St. Augustine; but his health giving way, he returned to Bruges, where, in July, he had a personal interview with Thomas More, Wolsey, and others, who were in favor with Henry VIII of England. He taught at Louvain during the winter semester of 1522–1523, after which, through the influence of the English dignitaries already mentioned, he was called to England.

In what capacity he went to England is hardly known. Some say as the tutor of King Henry's daughter Mary; others as a lecturer in the University

c

of Oxford. Certain it is that he gave two lectures at
Oxford, which were attended by the king and queen,
and that he received the honorary degree of D.C.L.,
in 1523. In 1526 appeared his treatise on the care of
the poor, which he dedicated to the municipal council
of Bruges. It was one of the first scientific treatments
of pauperism. He maintained that it was incumbent
upon State, and not upon the Church to care for the
poor. Buisson says of it, "Its suggestions are as
attractive as they are wise; and even to-day they
continue in full force."

In 1528 he published his pedagogic classic on the
Christian education of women. The mother, says
Vives, like Cornelia, should regard her children as
her most precious jewels. She should nurse her own
children because of possible physical influences on the
child. The mother should instruct her girl in all that
pertains to the household; and early teach her to read.
She should relate to her stories, not empty fables, but
such as will instruct and edify her and teach her to
love virtue and hate vice. The mother should teach
her daughter that riches, power, praise, titles, and
beauty are vain and empty things; and that piety,
virtue, bravery, meekness, and culture are imperish-
able virtues. Strong discipline in the home is urged.
Lax discipline, says Vives, makes a man bad, but it
makes a woman a criminal. Dolls should be banished
from the nursery because they encourage vanity and
love of dress. Boys and girls should not be instructed
together, not even during the earliest years of childhood. But women require to be educated as well as
men. This work, which presented in stronger terms
than hitherto the claims of the education of women,

was dedicated to Catherine of Aragon.   It was widely republished and had large influence.

For five years Vives had been a distinguished figure at the court of Henry VIII, but with the king's application for divorce, in 1528, came a rupture of these pleasant relations.   In a letter to a friend he says: "You must have heard of the troubles between the king and the queen, as it is now talked of everywhere. I have taken the side of the queen, whose cause has seemed to me just, and have defended her by word and pen.   This offended his Majesty to such degree that I was imprisoned for six weeks, and only released upon condition that I would never appear in the palace again.   I then concluded it safest to return home [to Bruges]; and, indeed, the queen advised me to in a secret letter.   Shortly after Cardinal Campeggio was sent to Britain to judge the cause.   The king was very solicitous that the queen appoint counsel to defend her side before Campeggio and Wolsey.   She, therefore, called me to her aid; but I told her plainly that any defence before such a court was useless, and that it would be much better to be condemned unheard, than with the *appearance* of defence.   The king sought only to save appearances with his people, that the queen might not appear to have been unjustly treated; but he had little regard for the rest.   At this the queen was incensed that I did not obey her call instead of following my own good judgment, which is worth more to me than all the princes of the world together. So it has come about that the king regards me as his adversary, and the queen regards me as disobedient and opinionated; and both of them have withdrawn my pension."

His closing years were passed at Bruges with his
wife's family; at Breda with the Duchess of Nassau,
a Spanish lady who had formerly been his pupil; and
at Paris, where he gave some courses of lectures.   He
had struggled against a weak constitution all his life,
and after his return from England other diseases
developed.   He died on May 6, 1540, in his forty-
eighth year, and was buried in the Church of St.
Donat at Bruges.

His most considerable contribution to the philosophy of education appeared after his return from England.   It was entitled *De disciplinis;* was published in
three parts, in 1531; and was dedicated to the King of
Portugal.   As Dr. Lange remarks, this work alone
entitles Vives to large consideration as an educational
reformer.

Vives justifies, in the introduction, the position he
assumes in regard to Aristotle; while he regards the
Greek as a great philosopher, he declares that the
world has gained in experience since Aristotle wrote,
and he sees no reason why his teachings should not be
set aside if found to be incorrect.   He has no doubt
but that later generations will find theories better
adapted to their ends than those he himself advocates,
but he greets as a friend the one who shall point out
his errors.

In the first part he treats of the decline of the
sciences. The causes of this decline he considers twofold: (1) Moral; and here he notes an unwillingness
to search for truth for truth's sake.   Pride is the root
of this evil.   A student in the University of Paris had
remarked to him, "Sooner than not distinguish myself
by founding some new doctrine, I would defend one of

whose falsity I was convinced." This moral weakness
he thought altogether inconsistent with the advancement of the sciences.   (2) Historical and material,
including as causes the migration of nations by which
existing orders of civilization have been annihilated;
the obscurity of ancient manuscripts, requiring more
time to decipher their meaning than it would take to
discover from nature their meaning; the ever increas-
ing use of commentaries in the study of originals, in
which the diverse opinions of the commentators lead
farther from the original sense; the practice of scholastic disputation which is taught the pupils before
they know what they are disputing about; and the
practice of regarding teaching as a trade rather than
a profession, thus causing many bright minds to select
other vocations, and to bring to the work incompetent
and coarse minds.

The second part treats of the decline of grammar,
and the third part of the art of teaching, in which he
gives some most sane directions.   Schools should be
located in the most healthy part of the community.
They should not be too near commercial centres; at
the same time, they should not be too distant from the
centre of population.   As to teachers, they should
have good academic training; they should be skilled
in the art of imparting knowledge; and their morals
should be such as would furnish examples to their
pupils.   Covetousness and ambition, above all things,
should be unknown to them.   Teachers who have
ambition and reputation in their minds are thereby
unfitted for the work of teaching.   On this account,
the state should fix the salaries, and the compensation
should be the wage of honest men.   There should be

a school in every community. Before pupils should be assigned tasks, teachers should ascertain their mental capacities and characteristics. They should also be privately tested four times a year; and when children are found who possess no taste for study they should be dismissed from the school. Corporal punishment should seldom be applied, and never to such a degree as to humiliate the pupils. Children should be given plenty of play time; and hearty, romping games are especially recommended. In the matter of method, Vives heartily commends the inductive, — from particulars to generals, — and he urges such a grouping of studies that each new subject studied may naturally grow out of the preceding lesson. While he strongly advises the study of the natural sciences, he is less enthusiastic here than Bacon, fearing, as he admits, that a contemplation of nature may prove dangerous to those not deeply grounded in faith.

But Vives was essentially a realist in his doctrines of education; and when his views are compared with those of Comenius, community of ideas is at once apparent. Both would begin education in the home and make the mother the first teacher. Both realized the need of better organization and classification of the schools. Both urged reforms in the matter of language teaching. Both considered education a matter of state concern, and urged pedagogical training for teachers. Both presented the claims of science and urged the coördination and correlation of the different subjects of study. Both emphasized the value of play and the need of physical training. Both advocated education for all classes of both sexes, and both exaggerated the need and importance of the religious training of the child.

Bacon

"Though there were many before Bacon, and especially artists and craftsmen," says Raumer, "who lived in communion with nature, and who, in manifold ways, transfigured and idealized her, and unveiled her glory; and, though their sense for nature was so highly cultivated that they attained to a practical understanding of her ways, yet this understanding was at best merely instinctive: for it led them to no scientific deductions and yielded them no thoughtful and legitimate dominion over her."

The founder of modern realism was born in London on the 22d of January in the year 1561. When sixteen years of age he entered Trinity College, Cambridge, where he studied under Dr. John Whitgift, a noted professor of theology, and afterward archbishop of Canterbury. He studied diligently the writings of Aristotle, but was convinced of their inadequacy. Writing of this period he says: "Amid men of sharp and strong wits, and abundance of leisure, and small variety of reading, their wits being shut up in the cells of a few authors, chiefly Aristotle, their dictator, as their persons are shut up in the cells of monasteries and colleges; and who knowing little history, either of nature or time, did out of no great quantity of matter, and infinite agitation of wit, spin cobwebs of learning, admirable for the fineness of the thread and work, but of no substance or profit."

The checkered career of Bacon is extraneous to his writings and may be passed over in silence. As noted in the first chapter, the educational institutions of the sixteenth century concerned themselves wholly with the acquisition and display of Latin eloquence. Grammar was studied with infinite labor and sorrow for years that students might acquire correct forms of speech; logic that they might express themselves with precision; and a minimum of history was taught that ancient records might furnish ornate illustrations in speaking and writing.

Erasmus and Melanchthon had disputed this ideal of culture, but it remained for Bacon to demolish this idol of mediævalism. "Forsooth," he says, "we suffer the penalty of our first parents' sin, and yet follow in their footsteps. They desired to be like God, and we, their posterity, would be so in a higher degree. For we create worlds, direct and control nature, and, in short, square all things by the measure of our own folly, not by the plummet of divine wisdom, nor as we find them in reality. I know not whether, for this result we are forced to do violence to nature or to our own intelligence the most; but it nevertheless remains true, that we stamp the seal of our own image upon the creatures and works of God, instead of carefully searching for, and acknowledging, the seal of the Creator manifest in them. Therefore have we lost, the second time, and that deservedly, our empire over the creatures, yea, when after and notwithstanding the fall, there was left to us some title to dominion over the unwilling creatures, so that they could be subjected and controlled, even this we have lost, in great part through our pride, in that we have desired to be like God, and to follow the dictates of our own reason alone. Now then, if there be any humility in the presence of the Creator, if there be any reverence for and exaltation of his handiwork, if there be any charity toward men, any desires to relieve the woes and sufferings of humanity, any love for the light of truth, and hatred toward the darkness of error, — I would beseech men again and again, to dismiss altogether, or at least for a moment to put away their absurd and intractable theories, which give to assumptions the dignity of hypotheses, dispense with experiment, and turn them away from the works of God. Let them with a teachable spirit approach the great volume of creation, patiently decipher its secret characters, and converse with its lofty truths; so shall they leave behind the delusive echoes of prejudice, and dwell within the perpetual outgoings of divine wisdom. This is that speech and language whose lines have gone out into all the earth, and no confusion of tongues has ever befallen it. This language we should all strive to understand, first condescending, like little children, to master its alphabet."

Instead of training children to interrogate nature for themselves, and to interpret the answers to these interrogations, instead of going straight to nature herself, the schools are forever teaching what others have thought and written on the subject. This procedure, according to Bacon, not only displays lack of pedagogic sense, but gives evidence of ignorance and self-conceit, and inflicts the greatest injury on philosophy and learning. Such methods of instruction, moreover, tend to stifle and interrupt all inquiry. We must, says Bacon, "come as new-born children, with open and fresh minds, to the observation of nature. For it is no less true in this human kingdom of knowledge than in God's kingdom of heaven, that no man shall enter into it except as he becomes first as a little child."

Bacon's notion, as summarized by Raumer, was that
"man must put himself again in direct, close, and
personal contact with nature, and no longer trust to
the confused, uncertain, and arbitrary accounts and
descriptions of her historians and would-be inter-
preters. From a clear and correct observation and
perception of objects, their qualities, powers, etc.,
the investigator must proceed, step by step, till he
arrives at laws, and to that degree of insight that will
enable him to interpret the laws and to analyze the
processes of nature. To this end Bacon proffers to us
his new method — the method of induction. With
the aid of this method we attain to an insight into
the connection and natural relation of the laws of
matter, and thus, according to him, we are enabled
through this knowledge to make nature subservient to
our will."

This was, according to Comenius, the true key to the
human intellect. But he laments that Bacon should
have given us the key and failed to unlock the door to
the treasure-house. But Bacon did more than formu-
late the laws of scientific induction for pedagogic purposes: he made possible the enrichment of the courses
of study by the addition of a wide range of school
studies. His thrusts at the Latin and Greek, as the
sole exponents of culture, were telling in their effect
and made possible the recognition of the vernacular
themes in Comenius' day. "The wisdom of the
Greeks," he says, "was rhetorical; it expended itself
upon words, and it had little to do with the search
after truth." Speaking again of classical culture, he
says: "These older generations fell short of many of
our present knowledges; they know but a small part

of the world, and but a brief period of history. We, on the contrary, are acquainted with a far greater extent of the world, besides having discovered a new hemisphere, and we look back and survey long periods of history."

Bacon recognized great individual differences in the mental capacities of children, and he urged that these differences and special tastes be taken into account by the teachers. He says: "The natural bent of the individual minds should be so far encouraged that a student who shall learn all that is required of him may be allowed time in which to pursue a favorite study. And, furthermore, it is worth while to consider, and I think this point has not hitherto received the attention which its importance demands, that there are two distinct modes of training the mind to a free and appropriate use of its faculties. The one begins with the easiest, and so proceeds to the more difficult; the other, at the outset, presses the pupil with the more difficult tasks, and, after he has mastered these, turns him to pleasanter and easier ones: for it is one method to practise swimming with bladders, and another to practise dancing with heavy shoes. It is beyond all estimate how a judicious blending of these two methods will profit both the mental and the bodily powers. And so to select and assign topics of instruction as to adapt them to the individual capabilities of the pupils, — this, too, requires a special experience and judgment. A close observation and an accurate knowledge of the different natures of the pupils are due from teachers to the parents of these pupils, that they may choose an occupation in life for their sons accordingly. And note further, that not only does every one make more rapid progress in those studies to which his nature inclines him, but, again, that a natural disinclination, in whatever direction, may be overcome by the help of special studies. For instance, if a boy has a light, inattentive, inconstant spirit, so that he is easily diverted, and his attention cannot be readily fixed, he will find advantage in the mathematics, in which a demonstration must be commenced anew whenever the thought wanders even for a moment."

These citations will suggest parallels in the aims of the two great reformers. Both sought to introduce the student to nature at first hand. Both aimed to reorganize the sciences into one great body of coördinated knowledge. Both emphasized the value of the inductive method in the development of subjects of study. Bacon said: "A good method will solve all problems. A cripple on the right path will beat a racer on the wrong path." Said Comenius: "The secret of education lies in method." Again: "There is no difficulty in learning Latin: what we want is a good method."

Ratke

Although but little more than twenty years the senior of Comenius, Ratke's mental development was less tardy, so that when the Moravian was a young collegian at Herborn, Ratke was enjoying the full flush of popularity as an educational reformer. Born at Wilster in Holstein (Germany), in 1571, he trained in the gymnasium at Hamburg, and later studied philosophy at Rostock. Later he travelled in England and Holland; studied Hebrew and Arabic, and formulated the plan of education which made him famous as a reformer. He attached great value to his plan and expressed great unwillingness to divulge it without adequate remuneration. He made known his contemplated reforms at a diet of the German Empire, held at Frankfort on the 12th of May, 1612. They were threefold: (1) To teach Latin, Greek, or Hebrew, or any other language, to young or old in a very short time; (2) to establish schools in which the arts and sciences should be taught and extended; (3) to introduce a uniform speech throughout the empire, and, at the same time, uniform government and religion. He proposed to follow the order and course of nature, and teach first the mother-tongue, after this Hebrew and Greek, as being the tongues of the original text of the Bible, and, lastly, Latin.

Through the influence of the princes (and more especially by the encouragement of the Duchess Dorothea of Weimar), the plans of Ratke were submitted to a commission selected from the faculties of the universities at Jena and Giessen, — Professors Grawer, Brendel, Walther, and Wolf representing Jena and Professors Helwig and Jung, Giessen. The report was favorable to Ratke. Professor Helwig, who was one of the best linguists of his day, was the spokesman for Giessen, and he accepted Ratke's views with great enthusiasm. "By diligent reflection and long practice," he says, "Ratke has discovered a valuable method by which good arts and languages can be taught and studied more easily, quickly, and correctly than has been usual in the schools. Ratke's method is more practicable in the arts than in the sciences, since arts and sciences are by their nature consistent with themselves, while the languages, on the contrary, by long use have acquired many inaccuracies."

Professor Helwig commends especially the methodology in Ratke's plan, and urges that we must consider not only the knowledge to be imparted, but as well the method of imparting knowledge. He says: "Nature does much, it is true, but when art assists her, her work is much more certain and complete. Therefore it is necessary that there should be an especial art to which any one who desires to teach can adhere, so that he shall not teach by mere opinion and guess, nor by native instinct alone, but by the rules of his art; just as he who would speak correctly by the rules of grammar, and he who would sing correctly by the rules of music. This art of teaching, like the art of logic, applies to all languages, arts, and sciences. It discusses among other things how to distinguish among minds and gifts, so that the quicker may not be delayed, and that, on the contrary, those who are by nature not so quick may not remain behind; how and in what order to arrange the exercises; how to assist the understanding; how to strengthen the memory; how to sharpen the intellect without violence and after the true course of nature. This art of teaching, no less than other arts, has its fixed laws and rules, founded not only upon the nature and understanding of man, but upon the peculiarities of languages, arts, and sciences; and it admits of no ways of teaching which are not deduced from sure grounds and founded upon proof." The Jena professors were no less favorable with regard to this new art of teaching.

The influence of this report on the fame of Ratke

was far-reaching. The following year (1614) he was invited to Augsburg to reform the schools of that city. This invitation was the outgrowth of a study of his plan by David Höschel, the principal of St. Anne's School, and two other teachers appointed by the city to accompany him to Frankfort and aid him in the investigation. They reported that Ratke had so far explained his method to them that they were satisfied and pleased with it; and the invitation to Ratke promptly followed. Beyond a few monographs by the Augsburg disciples, based on his method, and inspired doubtless by his sojourn there, we are altogether without evidence of the success or failure of the reforms at Augsburg.

Early in 1616, Prince Ludwig of Anhalt-Gotha yielded to the persuasions of his sister, the Duchess Dorothea of Weimar, and invited Ratke to Gotha to organize the schools there in accordance with his views. He engaged to organize and supervise the schools and to instruct and train the teachers, but he bound the prince to exact from each teacher a promise not to divulge his method to any one.

A printing-office was established at Gotha to supply the books required by the new order. Fonts of type in six languages were imported from Holland, and four compositors and two pressmen were brought from Rostock and Jena. The people of Gotha were required by the prince to send their children to the schools organized by Ratke. Two hundred and thirty-one boys and two hundred and two girls were enrolled.

The school was graded into six classes. The mother-tongue was taught in the lowest classes; Latin was begun in the fourth, and Greek in the sixth. He required that the teacher in the lowest class should be a man of kind manners, and that he need know no language but the German. This scandalized the whole German nation. A schoolmaster ignorant of Latin! Critics appeared from the first with the most cogent reasons for distrusting the "new methods." But Ratke had the confidence of the prince, and all went merrily for a time. The instruction was simplified; and, besides the mother-tongue, arithmetic, singing, and religion were taught.

But he encountered numerous obstacles at Gotha: the teachers of the town, it would appear, did not fully share his views; the town adhered to the Reformed Church and Ratke was a Lutheran, — a fact which caused no end of trouble; and the prince was not altogether satisfied with the fulfilment of Ratke's promises of reform. The pastor of the Reformed Church of Gotha preferred formal charges of heterodoxy against him, and maintained, besides, that Ratke made too little provision for the study of music and the catechism; that too much time was given to recreation; that the discipline was altogether too mild; and that the children were permitted to pass from one study to another too rapidly. Singular charges, these! And the more singular when one recalls the long hours and the harsh discipline of the seventeenth century.

The opposition was strong, and at the end of eighteen months the Gotha experiment was brought to an abrupt close. Ratke was not only dismissed, but was imprisoned on the charge that he "had claimed and promised more than he knew that he could bring to pass." After spending the best of a year in prison,

he signed a declaration in which he assented to the
charges.   Then the prince released him.   He went to
Magdeburg, where he was well received by the school
authorities; but the ecclesiastical dignitaries of the
city were soon at war with him, and he moved on to
Rudolstadt, where he was cordially received by the
Princess Anna Sophia, wife of Prince Gunther of
Swarzburg-Rudolstadt.

Subsequently Oxenstiern, the chancellor of Sweden,
sought his services in the reformation of the Swedish
schools; but instead of the requested interview, he
sent the chancellor a thick quarto.   "I accomplished
this wearisome labor," says Oxenstiern; "and after I
had read the whole book through, I found that he had
not ill displayed the faults of the schools, but his
remedies did not seem to me adequate."   Ratke died
shortly afterward at the age of sixty-four years.

Ratke's contribution to education was chiefly in the
matter of methodology.   His leading principles were:
(1) In everything we should follow the order of nature.
There is a certain natural sequence along which the
human intelligence moves in the acquisition of knowledge.   This sequence must be studied, and instruction
must be based on a knowledge of it.   (2) One thing
at a time.   Each subject of study should be orderly
developed and thoroughly dealt with before proceeding
to the next.   (3) There should be frequent repetition.
It is astonishing what may be accomplished by the
frequent repetition of one thing.   (4) Everything first
in the mother-tongue.   The first thinking should
always be in the vernacular.   Whatever the vocation,
the pupil should learn to express himself in the
mother-tongue.   After the mother-tongue has been

D

mastered, the other languages may be studied.
(5) Everything without compulsion. Children cannot be whipped into learning or wishing to learn; by
compulsion and blows they are so disgusted with their
studies that study becomes hateful to them. Moreover, it is contrary to nature to flog children for not
remembering what has been taught them. If they
had been properly taught they would have remembered, and blows would have been unnecessary. Children should be taught to love and reverence — not to
fear their teachers. (6) Nothing should be learned by
rote. Learning by heart weakens the understanding.
If a subject has been well developed, and has been
impressed upon the mind by frequent repetition, the
memory of it will follow without any pains. Frequent hours of recreation are advised; in fact, no two
lessons should come immediately together. (7) A definite method (and a uniform method) for all studies.
In the languages, arts, and sciences, there must be a
conformity in the methods of teaching, text-books
used, and precepts given. The German grammar, for
instance, must agree with the Hebrew and the Greek
as far as the idioms of the language will permit.
(8) The thing itself should first be studied, and then
whatever explains it. Study first the literature of a
language and then its grammar. A basis of material
must first be laid in the mind before rules can be
applied. He admits that many of the grammars furnish examples with the rules; but these examples
"come together from all sorts of authors, like mixed
fodder in a manger." (9) Everything must be learned
by experience and examination. Nothing is to be
taken on authority. It will be recalled that Ratke

visited England after the completion of his studies at
Rostock; and it is altogether likely that while there
he became a convert to induction and the philosophy
of Bacon.

In most particulars Ratke and Comenius were in
harmony. Both urged that the study of things should
precede or be united with the study of words; that
knowledge should be communicated through appeals
to the senses; that all linguistic study should begin
with the mother-tongue; that methods of teaching
should be in accordance with the laws of nature; and
that progress in studies should be based not on
compulsion, but on the interest aroused in the pupils.

Campanella, Andreæ, and Bateus

Comenius derived many of his philosophic concepts
from the Dominican reformer, Thomas Campanella,
whose writings influenced him powerfully, at least
during his student years at Herborn and Heidelberg.
The writings of Campanella convinced him of the
unwisdom of the study of nature from the works of
Aristotle. Books, Campanella had declared, are but
dead copies of life, and are full of error and decep-
tion. We must ourselves explore nature and write
down our own thoughts, the living mirror which shows
the reflection of God's countenance. These protests
against scholasticism found a responsive chord in the
thoughts of the young Comenius.

In the preface to the *Prodromus* Comenius is unre-
served in his expression of obligations to his predecessors. "Who, indeed, should have the first place,"
he says, "but John Valentine Andreæ, a man of nimble

and clear brain." The court preacher of Stuttgart had strongly impressed Comenius by his deep love for Christian ideals and his warm enthusiasm for their realization in practical life, as well as by his humorous polemics against the dead scholasticism of his day. Comenius incorporates in his *Great didactic* a brief by Andreæ on "the use of the art of teaching," in which he maintains (1) that parents up to this time have been uncertain how much to expect from their children; (2) that schoolmasters, the greater number of whom have been ignorant of their art, have exhausted their energies and worn themselves out in their efforts to fulfil their duty; (3) that students should master the sciences without difficulty, tedium, or blows, as if in sport and in merriment; (4) that schools should become places of amusement, houses of delight and attraction, and the work so adjusted that students of whatever capacity might attain a high standard of development; (5) that states should exist for the development of the young; (6) that schools should be so efficient that the Church may never lack learned doctors, and the learned doctors lack suitable hearers; and (7) that the schools may be so reformed that they may give a more exact and universal culture of the intellect, and that Christian youths may be more fervently stirred up to vigor of mind and love of heavenly things. "Let none, therefore," says Andreæ, "withdraw his thoughts, desires, strength, and resources from such a sacred undertaking. It is inglorious to despair of progress and wrong to despise the counsel of others."

The obligation of Comenius to William Bateus, the Irish Jesuit, was not great, although he makes free acknowledgment of the same in the *Janua*. Indeed, the plan of the *Janua* was well formulated before he knew of the existence of the Jesuit father's book. He made known the plan of his *Janua* to some friends, who told him that Bateus had already published a similar work. He was not content until he had procured a copy of the book. "The idea," says Comenius, "was better than the execution. Nevertheless, as he was the prime inventor, I thankfully acknowledge it, nor will I upbraid him for those errors he has committed." This willing recognition of his obligation to a wide range of educational writers is proof of the declaration he often made, "I care not whether I act the part of teacher or learner."

CHAPTER III

Ancestry of Comenius — Attends the village school at Strasnitz — Studies Latin in the gymnasium at Prerau — Character of the Latin schools of his day — Enters the college at Herborn — Studies theology and philosophy — Inspired by the teachings of Alsted — Makes the acquaintance of the writings of Ratke — Continues his studies at Heidelberg — Begins his career as a teacher at Prerau — Ordained as a clergyman — Installed as pastor and school superintendent at Fulneck — Persecution.

MANY of the facts concerning the early life of John Amos Comenius are shrouded in obscurity. It is certain, however, that he was born in the village of Nivnitz in Moravia (now a province of Austria) on the 28th day of March, in the year 1592. Nivnitz then, as now, was little more than a country market town and settled quite largely by members of the religious organization known as Moravian Brethren. The father and mother of Comenius, Martin and Anna Komensky, were influential members of the brotherhood, who had settled here some years previous with other followers of John Hus, the Bohemian reformer and martyr. The tradition that Martin Komensky was a miller by trade does not seem to be well authenticated. Besides John Amos, three daughters were born to Martin and Anna Komensky, — Ludmilla, Susanna, and Margaret, — but the three girls died in early childhood.

Martin Komensky died in 1604,[1] and his wife sur-
vived him less than a year. Left an orphan at the
early age of twelve years, Comenius was intrusted to
the care and training of an improvident aunt, who
soon made way with his inheritance. In this, as
in the neglect of his school training, the incom-
petence of the foster parent is clearly apparent. For
something more than four years the lad attended
the village school at Strasnitz. But, as he himself
tells us, the curriculum was narrow and the teaching
poor. While here Comenius formed the acquaintance
of a schoolfellow named Nicholas Drabik, through
whose prophetic visions he was so ignominiously led
astray in his later life, and so bitterly reproached by
his contemporaries. "It was a strange irony of fate,"
remarks Mr. Keatinge, "that a wanderer like
Comenius, when only eleven years old and in his
native land, should commence the intimacy that was
to embitter his old age in Amsterdam." But, as Benham notes, the fact that the matter was so soon forgotten shows that the character of Comenius received
no indelible stain by the unfortunate alliance, even
though he excited the ridicule and disrespect, and
even the contempt, of his contemporaries.

At the advanced age of sixteen years, he was initiated into the mysteries of classical learning in the
Latin school at Prerau, where he studied for two
years. A fairly accurate notion of his studies during
this period may be gained from a glance at the course
of study in a contemporary Latin school herewith

[1] I am aware that Comenius says that his father died in 1602; but
the evidence which Vrbka has adduced seems to me conclusive that
the senior Komensky died two years later.

reproduced in translation from the Bohemian.[1] The schedule of hours in the second grade of this school was as follows: In the morning, during the first hour, repetition of grammar lesson from memory and explanation of the next day's grammar lesson. During the second hour, the dialogues of Castalio; and the third hour, the recitation of Castalio's dialogues in the Bohemian, and the grammatical analysis of the words and conversation of the lesson. In the afternoon, during the first hour, writing and singing; the second hour, explanation of the writings of Cicero according to Sturm's edition, and grammatical analysis; and the third hour, exercises in words and sayings. This was the programme for Mondays, Tuesdays, Thursdays, and Saturdays. On Wednesdays there was but one lesson in the morning and one in the afternoon. In the morning the catechism was recited; in addition, imitative exercises for the formation of style. In the afternoon, the writing of short words and a recapitulation of the week's lessons.

The programme for the third grade was as follows: In the forenoon of Mondays, Tuesdays, Thursdays, and Fridays: —

First hour. — Repetition of Latin rules in the mother-tongue.

Second hour. — Exposition of the conversations of John Lewis Vives.

Third hour. — Repetition of the above, and Bohemian exercises from the text.

In the afternoon of the same days, first hour, writing and singing; second hour, Greek grammar and the

[1] *Rukovét Skolstvi Obecného.* By Karel Toubenek and Karel Vorovka. Prague, 1892. Translated by Miss Clara Vostrovsky.

collected writings of John Sturm; and third hour, exposition of Greek proverbs from the New Testament, together with grammatical analysis of the same. This class had for its forenoon lesson on Wednesdays the catechism and exercises in the Bohemian, and in the afternoon singing and writing. *In the summer the more industrious pupils were excused from the lessons on Wednesday afternoons.*

One period on Saturday was devoted to a weekly review; and on Sunday morning a chapter was read from the New Testament, the same explained in Greek (to all grades above the second), and all the students attended church. In the afternoon there was preaching again and more reading from the New Testament.

Such we may suppose to have been the character of his studies at Prerau during the two years from 1608 to 1610. Because of his maturity, he appreciated most keenly the faults of current humanistic methods of teaching. As one of his biographers remarks: "The defects of this early education were the seeds from which sprang the whole of his didactic efforts. Considerably older than his schoolfellows, he was able to criticise the methods and speedily arrive at the conclusion that the lack of progress was due more to the inefficiency of the teachers than to the idleness of their pupils. From this time onward, he began to devise new methods of class instruction and better schemes of study. From the vivid memory of the horrors through which he had passed, of the thousand and one rules that had to be learned by rote before they were understood, of the monotonous study of grammar, only diversified by the maddening effort to translate Latin authors without the assistance of suitable dictionaries or commentaries, sprang that intense sympathy with beginners which characterizes his whole life and gives practical worth to every precept that he enunciated."

After two years in the Latin school at Prerau, he entered the college at Herborn on the 30th of March, 1611. The University of Prague was at this time in the hands of the Utraquists, whose unfriendly attitude toward the Moravian Brethren led to the selection of a German university for his higher course of instruction. He had determined to qualify for the ministry, and the institution at Herborn at this time afforded unusual opportunities for the study of theology. Doubtless another factor in the selection of Herborn was the fact that John Henry Alsted, one of the most distinguished theological and philosophical professors of the day, was lecturing there, and aspiring youths of the temperament of Comenius naturally gravitated toward this centre of fresh thought. Although but four years older than Comenius, Alsted was the most commanding figure in the academic circles of Europe at this time. He had travelled extensively; had made the acquaintance of most of the learned men in Europe worth knowing; and had advocated views of education which were new and startling.

For twenty-seven years Herborn had enjoyed unprecedented academic prosperity. Opportunities for the study of education were unexcelled; for, connected with the college, there was a preparatory department which served as a laboratory for the study of pedagogic problems, in which, for example, the lower classes were instructed in the mother-tongue — a procedure that was regarded as ultra-heterodox at this time.

Comenius was most helped by the instruction of the distinguished theologian and philosopher, Professor John Henry Alsted. The teachings of Alsted were of a character calculated to deepen the convictions of the young student from Moravia, for the Herborn professor taught among other things — as is indicated by his *Encyclopœdia of the sciences,* published a few years later — the following: (1) Not more than one thing should be taught at a time; (2) not more than one book should be used on one subject, and not more than one subject should be taught on one day; (3) everything should be taught through the medium of what is more familiar; (4) all superfluity should be avoided; (5) all study should be mapped out in fixed periods; (6) all rules should be as short as possible; (7) everything should be taught without severity, though discipline must be maintained; (8) corporal punishment should be reserved for moral offences, and never inflicted for lack of industry; (9) authority should not be allowed to prejudice the mind against the facts gleaned from experience, nor should custom or preconceived opinion prevail; (10) the construction of a new language should first be explained in the vernacular; (11) no language should be taught by means of grammar; (12) grammatical terms should be the same in all languages. "The teacher," said Alsted, "should be a skilled reader of character, so that he may be able to classify the dispositions of his pupils. Unless he pays great attention to differences of disposition, he will but waste all the efforts he expends in teaching."

Another professor of philosophy at Herborn at the time was Heinrich Gutberleth, who was likewise deeply interested in pedagogy and whose lectures

seem to have influenced Comenius, with special reference to his advocacy of the study of the physical
sciences.   In theology he heard lectures by Piscator,
Hermannus, and Pasor.   Since 1530 the schools of
Nassau had been marked by great improvement, and
this improvement was in no small measure due to the
intelligent interest of the professors of theology at
Herborn in the schools of the province.   Hermannus,
with whom Comenius studied practical theology, was
especially active in school reform.

It was during his student life at Herborn that
Comenius became acquainted with Ratke's plan of
instruction, then much discussed at university centres,
and especially at Jena, Giessen, and Herborn.   However much he may have been stimulated to educational
reform by his own belated classical training and by
the pedagogic character of the work at Herborn, the
writings of Ratke, as he himself tells us, played the
largest part in making him an educational reformer.
While at Herborn he gave special attention to the
Bohemian language, and planned a dictionary which
was never published.

Comenius left Herborn in the spring of 1613; and
after a few weeks' sojourn at Amsterdam he repaired
to Heidelberg, where he matriculated as a student of
philosophy and theology on the 13th of June.   Beyond
the fact that he purchased a manuscript of Copernicus,
and that at the end of a year, his funds becoming
exhausted, he was forced to make the return journey
to Prague on foot, nothing is known of his life at
Heidelberg.

Back in his native country after these years of study
and travel in Germany, he was still too young by two

years for ordination in the brotherhood.   Meanwhile
he turned his attention to education, and engaged himself as a teacher in the elementary school at Prerau
conducted by the Moravian Brethren.   This experience brought him face to face with problems of methodology and discipline, and gave him an opportunity to
apply some of the theories he had formulated while a
student at Herborn.   His attention was at once called
to the ineffective methods employed in teaching Latin,
for the remedy of which he prepared an easy Latin
book for beginners.

His ordination took place at Zerwick on the 29th
day of April, 1616, although he continued teaching at
Prerau for two years longer, when he was called to
the pastorate of the flourishing Moravian church at
Fulneck.   At the same time, or shortly thereafter, he
was elected superintendent of the schools of the town.
In this twofold capacity he ministered to the spiritual
and educational needs of Fulneck for three years, and
passed the only tranquil and happy years of his life.
But the year that ushered in this prosperous career
witnessed the outbreak of the Thirty Years' War.

In 1621 Fulneck was sacked by the Spaniards, and
the conquering force gave itself up to destruction that
baffles description.   Houses were pillaged, including
the residence of Comenius, and he lost all his property, including his library and the manuscripts of
several educational treatises, on the composition of
which he had spent years of labor.

From this time on, the Moravian Brethren were
exposed to the most relentless persecutions.   Many
were executed, and others took refuge in caves in the
wilderness or on the secluded estates of wealthy sym-

pathizers. For three years Comenius found an asylum
on the estate of Karl von Zerotin. The death of his
wife and children (for he had married while at Fulneck) added to the afflictions of his exile; but he
sought relief from his sorrow in literary work — the
composition of a metrical translation of the Psalms, an
allegorical description of life, and the construction of
a highly meritorious map of Moravia.

The persecution of the enemies rendered concealment no longer possible; and, although Karl von
Zerotin was held in high regard by Ferdinand II, in
1624 the imperial mandate was issued which banished
the evangelical clergy from the country. For a time
Comenius and several of his brethren secreted themselves from their merciless pursuers on the Bohemian
mountains, in the citadel of Baron Sadowsky, near
Slaupna. But the edict of 1627 put an end to further
protection of the Moravian clergy by the nobles; and
in January, 1628, Comenius and many of his compatriots, including his late protector, Baron Sadowsky,
set out for Poland. On the mountain frontier which
separates Moravia from Silesia, one gets an excellent
view of Fulneck and the surrounding country. Here
the band of exiles knelt and Comenius offered up an
impassioned prayer for his beloved Moravia and Bohemia. This was his last sad look on his devoted country. He never afterward beheld the land of his
fathers, but for more than half a century he lived an
exile in foreign regions. Well might he, in his old
age, exclaim: "My whole life was merely the visit of
a guest; I had no fatherland."

CHAPTER IV

Flight to Poland — Appointed director of the gymnasium at Lissa —
Reforms introduced — Literary projects — Need of a patron —
Call to England — Friendship with Hartlib — Interest of the Eng-
lish Parliament — Discontent with existing educational institu-
tions — Lewis de Geer, his Dutch patron — Call to Sweden —
Interview with Oxenstiern — Located at Elbing — Reform of the
Swedish schools — Return to Poland — Consecration as senior
bishop — Consequences of the treaty of Westphalia — Ecclesiasti-
cal ministrations — Call to Hungary — Reform of the schools at
Saros-Patak — Plan of a pansophic school — Return to Lissa —
The city burned — Flight of Comenius from Poland.

AFTER the flight from Bohemia, Comenius and his
compatriots found a refuge at Lissa, Poland, with
Count Raphael, a powerful prince of the faith of the
Moravian Brethren, to whose estate hundreds of per-
secuted Bohemians had already fled. Twelve years
were passed in Lissa, during which time Comenius
was actively engaged in educational reform. Besides
the composition of three of his most important books
— the *Janua*, in 1631, the *Great didactic*, probably in
1632, and the *School of infancy*, in 1633 — he engaged
actively in the work of teaching. A secondary school
of acknowledged repute had been maintained in Lissa
by the Moravian Brethren since 1555, and here
Comenius found the opportunity of putting into practice some of his educational theories. It is apparent,
however, from his writings, that he read widely before

47

undertaking the reorganization of the gymnasium at Lissa, and that he sought aid from all the writers on education, both ancient and modern. His correspondents at this period included such distinguished names as Lubin, Andreæ, Ritter, Vogel, Ratke, Frey, Mencel, Hartlib, Evenius, Johnstone, and Mochinger. To these distinguished contemporaries he expresses his dissatisfaction with current educational practices, and seeks guidance in the reform movement he has instituted in Poland.

"When our people attend school for the sake of the learned languages, what do they bring with them on returning home?" he asks. "What beyond that which they obtain there — the tinkling of human eloquence, the love of disputation, and the knowledge that puffeth up instead of the charity that buildeth up. Moreover, some acquire corrupt morals; some, a desire to make themselves agreeable by a show of external civility; some, habits of intemperance and a distaste or hatred of firm discipline. And yet these very men were trained for the lights of the Church and the pillars of the State. O that, instead of such an education, we had retained the simplicity of childhood. O that we might bring back the ancient custom of the Spartans, who, more than all the other Greeks, were intent upon the rational education of their youth."

A noteworthy feature of his work as a reformer at Lissa consisted in a careful grading of the schools, and the formulation of a course of study for the successive grades. The guiding principle in this schematization of school work was that each grade should pave the way for the one next higher, — the elements of all subjects of study being comparatively simple, these

elements should be gradually introduced and elaborated from grade to grade. These reforms were not
only far-reaching, they were revolutionary; and they
made possible the modern graded school.

Civilized Europe did not long remain in ignorance
of these reforms. They were discussed with approval
in England, Germany, France, and Sweden; and several foreign governments sought his services in the
work of educational reform. Sweden, in 1638, ten-
dered him a remunerative position and unlimited
opportunities of reforming the schools of the kingdom
along the lines laid down in his writings. He replied
that he was willing to recommend a competent person
to undertake the work, but that he was not in position
to sever his relations with the Moravian Church in
Poland and to leave unfinished some important
educational writings.

His own poverty, as well as that of his brethren,
made him realize keenly the need of a wealthy patron
to aid him in the realization of his educational ideals.
"The vastness of the labors I contemplate," he wrote,
"demands that I should have a wealthy patron,
whether we look at their extent, or at the necessity of
securing assistants, or at the expense generally. I
propose to render the study of science, philosophy,
and theology more accessible to all parties, and of
greater usefulness in the regulation of human affairs
than has hitherto been the case. In order to do this,
two kinds of books are necessary — (1) for philosophical research and (2) for elementary training.

"Books of the first class would primarily have reference to the Latin language, and of this class I would
adopt eight: —

E

"1. The *Vestibulum*, or introduction to the Latin tongue.

"2. The *Janua*, or gate of the Latin tongue.

"3. The *Palace*, or essentials of the Latin language.

"4. A dictionary giving the meaning of the Latin words in the mother-tongue.

"5. A dictionary giving all the words of the native language in Latin, and more especially supplying phrases of the former language with corresponding phrases in the latter.

"6. A Latin dictionary explaining all the peculiar idioms of the language.

"7. An elementary grammar containing all the declensions and conjugations, and to be used in connection with the *Vestibulum*.

"8. A more comprehensive grammar, to be used in connection with the *Janua*.

"The books to be used in connection with elementary training are three: —

"1. *Pansophia*, or universal wisdom. This book should comprise the sum total of human wisdom, and be so expressed as to meet the requirements of both the present and future ages. The method to be followed in such a book would be to reduce it to certain fundamental principles, beyond the compass of which no part of human knowledge can reach. Such first principles are God, the world, and common sense.

"2. *Panhistoria*, or universal history. This work must comprehend the most vital facts of all ages. Universal history is a most excellent handmaid of the understanding, searching into the causes of all things, and inquiring into the laws of cause and effect. Instruction in history must be graded. It might be arranged in six classes — Bible history, natural history, history of inventions, history of morals, history of the various religious rites, and general history.

"3. General dogmatics.   These have to treat of the different theories taken by human ingenuity, the false as well as the true, thereby preventing a relapse into vain speculations and dangerous errors.

"One man is not able to accomplish an undertaking of such magnitude.   There ought to be some clever linguists, perhaps three well versed in philosophy, an able historian, and a man thoroughly acquainted with Biblical literature.   As regards the philological labors, I have already met with an excellent assistant in Mr. Wechner.   Nor are clever coadjutors wanting for the *Pansophia,* who have not only offered the treasures of their libraries, but who have offered themselves in their coöperation in this work.   Among these my friend Hartlib far excels.   I do not know his equal in the extent of his knowledge, his acuteness of reasoning, his zeal to become useful to the welfare of mankind, his fervent love for a philosophy unmixed with errors and fanciful speculations, and his self-denial in order to further the objects in view."

Such a patron, however, was not at once forthcoming, although it would appear from his letters that Count Bohulslaw of Lissa, whom he styles "the chief in the kingdom of Poland," was of some pecuniary assistance to him at this time in the development of his theories.

The wide publication of his writings aroused a keen interest in his reforms, and especially in England. Samuel Hartlib, who corresponded extensively with the learned men of Europe, had already translated into English several of the educational writings of

Comenius, and in various other ways had interested the English public in the work of the Moravian reformer.

The keen personal interest of Hartlib in the work of Comenius had important temporary consequences on the direction of the reformer's activities during the next few years. Hartlib at this time was the most interesting figure in English educational history. "Everybody knew him," says Professor Masson.[1] "He was a foreigner by birth, being the son of a Polish merchant who had left Poland when the country fell under Jesuit rule, and had settled in Elbing in Prussia, in very good circumstances. Twice married before to Polish ladies, this merchant had married in Prussia for his third wife the daughter of a wealthy English merchant at Dantzig; and thus our Hartlib, their son, though Prussian born and with Polish connections, could reckon himself half English. The date of his birth was probably about the beginning of the century. He appears to have first visited England in or about 1628, and from that time, though he made frequent journeys to the continent, London had been his headquarters. Here, with a residence in the city, he carried on business as a merchant, with extensive foreign correspondence, and very respectable family connections. But it did not require such family connections to make Hartlib at home in English society. The character of the man would have made him at home anywhere. He was one of those persons now styled philanthropists, or friends of progress, who take an interest in every question or project of their

[1] *The life of John Milton.* By David Masson. Vol. III. London, 1873.

time promising social improvement, have always some irons in the fire, are constantly forming committees, or writing letters to persons of influence, and live altogether for the public.   By the common consent of all who have explored the intellectual and social history of England in the seventeenth century, he is one of the most interesting and memorable figures of that whole period.   He is interesting both for what he did himself and on account of the number and intimacy of his contacts with other interesting people."

Through Hartlib's influence the English Parliament invited Comenius to England.   This was in the summer of 1641.   Comenius himself may be permitted to tell how all this came about: "After my *Pansophia* had been published and dispersed through the various countries of Europe, many learned men approved of the object and plan of the work, but despaired of its ever being acccomplished by one man alone, and therefore advised that a college of learned men should be instituted to carry it into effect.   Mr. Samuel Hartlib, who had forwarded its publication in England, labored earnestly in this matter, and endeavored by every possible means to bring together for this purpose a number of intellectual men.   And at length, having found one or two, he invited me with many strong entreaties.   As my friends consented to my departure, I proceeded to London, and arrived there on the autumnal equinox (September the 22d) in the year 1641, and then learned that I had been called thither by an order of the Parliament.   But, in consequence of the king having gone to Scotland, the Parliament had been dismissed for three months, and, consequently, I had to winter in London."

His friends meanwhile examined with more detail
his educational views and encouraged him to elaborate
his views in a tract, which he named *Via lucis,* or the
way of light.   This, as he himself says, was "a national disquisition as to the manner in which wisdom
— the intellectual law of minds — may at length
toward the evening of the world be felicitously dif-
fused through all minds in all nations."

Around Comenius Hartlib soon collected a group of
thoughtful men interested in the Moravian reformer's
views; and together we may suppose they discussed
at length the larger educational problems already
formulated by Comenius in his published writings.
The group included, besides Hartlib, Mr. John Pell,
a mathematician of acknowledged repute; John Milton, the poet and educational writer; Theodor Haak,
the expositor of philosophic systems; John Wilkins,
the agricultural enthusiast; John Durie, the advocate
of evangelical unity; Thomas Farnaby, the schoolmaster at Sevenoaks and one of the English editors
of Comenius' *Janua;* and probably the American
Winthrop, later governor of Connecticut, who was
wintering in London.   He was delighted with London
and the people he met.   Writing to friends in Lissa,
he says: "I live as a friend among friends; though
not so many visit me as would if they knew that I
could speak English, or if they had more confidence
in their own Latin."

When Parliament finally convened "and my presence being known," writes Comenius, "I was com-
manded to wait until after some important business
having been transacted, a commission should be issued
to certain wise and learned Englishmen to hear me

and be informed of my plan. As an earnest, moreover, of their intentions, they communicated to me their purpose to assign to us a college with revenues, whence some men of learning and industry selected from any nation might be honorably sustained either for a certain number of years or in perpetuity. The Savoy in London, and beyond London, Winchester, and again near the city, Chelsea, were severally mentioned, and inventories of the latter and its revenues were communicated to me; so that nothing seemed more certain than that the designs of Lord Bacon to open a universal college of all nations, devoted solely to the advancement of the sciences, were now in way of being carried into effect."

Comenius had assumed that when the call to England came to him at Lissa, it simply represented a private movement backed by Hartlib and other influential Englishmen; and he expresses himself in terms of delighted surprise upon arriving in London to find that he had been summoned thither by the Parliament of the realm. The parliamentary sanction of this summons has never been corroborated. Professor Masson made the attempt, but was unable to find in the Lords' or Commons' *Journal* for the years 1641 and 1642 any traces of communication between Comenius and the Parliament of which he speaks. He admits that there may be such corroborative evidence, since the indexes for these years are incomplete. There are, however, no good and sufficient reasons for doubting the word of Comenius in this matter.

There are traces at this period of parliamentary dissatisfaction with current English education, and more particularly with university education in England. Professor Masson thus states the matter: "There had for some time been a tradition of dissatisfaction with the existing state of the universities and the great public schools. In especial, Bacon's complaints and suggestions in the second book of his *De Augmentis* had sunk into thoughtful minds. That the universities, by persistence in old and outworn methods, were not in full accord with the demands and needs of the age; that their aims were too professional and particular, and not sufficiently scientific and general; that the order of studies in them was bad, and some of the studies barren; that there ought to be a bold direction of their endowments and apparatus in the line of experimental knowledge, so as to extract from nature new secrets and sciences for which humanity was panting; that, moreover, there ought to be more fraternity and correspondence among the universities of Europe and some organization of their labors, with a view to mutual illumination and collective advancement: — all these Verulamian speculations, first submitted to King James, were lying here and there in English intellects in watch for an opportunity."

But the time was not yet come for the reform movement in English education. Ireland was in a state of commotion; two hundred thousand Englishmen had been massacred;[1] the sudden departure of the king from London on the 10th of January, 1642, and the prospect of a prolonged civil war convinced Comenius that it would be useless to tarry longer in England. He informed his friends of his disappointment of his plans. Hartlib was hopeful and urged delay, but a

[1] Professor Masson.

call to Sweden, made four years previous, was renewed at this time, and he left London on the 10th of June, in the year 1642.

Lewis de Geer, a rich Dutch merchant and philanthropist, residing at Nordköping, Sweden, had offered to render him financial aid in working out his educational reforms in Sweden. But de Geer's notions of reform differed widely from those of the English friends. He was less interested in universal research, the founding of pansophic colleges, and the results of original investigation than Hartlib and the Englishmen. What he wanted was better schoolbooks for the children, rational methods of teaching for the teachers, and some intelligent grading of the schools. The English friends were satisfied with the broad generalities of pansophic learning, the unrealized dreams that were so very near the reformer's heart; the Dutch merchant would be satisfied with nothing less than concrete applications of theories. There is no doubt that Comenius would have preferred lingering in England or going to some place where his cherished pansophic schemes might be given a hearing. But he was human and had organic needs, and he knew that the liberal remuneration offered him by de Geer would avert poverty even though the realization of his pure and exalted pansophic dream was deferred.

"In the history of great renunciations," says Mr. Keatinge,[1] "surely none is stranger than this. We have a man little past the prime of life, his brain

---

[1] *The Great didactic of John Amos Comenius.* With introductions, biographical and historical. By M. W. Keatinge. London, 1896. pp. 468.

teeming with magnificent, if somewhat visionary, plans for social reform, a mighty power in the community that shared his religious ideas, and an object of interest even to those who may have shrugged their shoulders at his occasional want of balance. Suddenly he flings his projects to the winds, consigns his darling plans to the dustheap of unrealizable ideas, and retires to a small seaside town — not to meditate, not to give definite form to latent conceptions or to evolve new ones, not to make preparation for the dazzling of intellectual Europe with an octavo of fantastic philanthropy or of philosophic mysticism, but — to write school-books for the little boys in Swedish schools."

Comenius went from London to Nordköping, where he spent some days in conference with his new patron, Lewis de Geer. He was not to receive a stipulated salary, but to be paid certain sums upon the completion of definite texts, the number and character of the same to be determined by the educational authorities at Stockholm, whither de Geer directed Comenius to go for further orders. In Stockholm he met with Lord Axel Oxenstiern, grand chancellor of the kingdom of Sweden, and Dr. John Skyte, professor of canon and civil law (as well as chancellor) in the University of Upsala. Of this conference Comenius says: "These two exercised me in debate for four days, and chiefly Oxenstiern, that eagle of the north. He inquired into the foundations of both my schemes, the didactic and the pansophic, so searchingly that it was unlike anything that had been done before by any of my learned critics. In the first two days he examined the didactics, with, at length, this conclusion: 'From

an early age,' said he, 'I perceived that our method
of studies generally in use is a harsh and crude one,
but where the root of the trouble was I couldn't find
out.   At length having been sent by my king [Gus-
tavus Adolphus], of glorious memory, as ambassador
into Germany, I conversed on the subject with various
learned men.   And when I heard that Wolfgang Ratke
was toiling at a reformed method, I had no rest of mind
until I had got that gentleman into my presence; but,
instead of a talk on the subject, he offered me a big
volume in quarto to read.   I swallowed that trouble;
and, having gone through the book, I noted that he
detected not badly the maladies of the schools; but
the remedies he proposed did not seem to me sufficient.
Yours, Mr. Comenius, rest on firmer foundations.' "[1]

The consultation with Oxenstiern and Skyte continued four days, at the conclusion of which they rendered their decision on his various theories.   With
reference to his pansophic notions, they saw little of
immediate utility to the welfare of mankind.   But his
didactics they regarded with favor.   They urged him
to give his attention to the reformation of teaching
and the preparation of suitable text-books.   While
somewhat chagrined at this unsympathetic attitude
toward his pansophic theories, and a little surprised
to learn that de Geer should be of the same mind, he
was forced to acquiesce, not, however, without the earnest solicitations of Hartlib and his English friends
not to forsake the cherished pansophic principles.[2]

[1] *Mittheilungen über Wolfgang Ratichius.*   Von Agathon
Niemeyer.   Halle, 1840.

[2] In a letter to Governor Winthrop of Connecticut, Hartlib laments that Comenius should continually allow himself to be diverted
from his pansophic works.

The town of Elbing, on the Baltic Sea, in West Prussia, was designated by de Geer as a suitable residence for Comenius during the time that he should be in the service of the Swedish educational department. Here he settled, with his family and the assistants de Geer had permitted him to employ at the patron's expense, in October, 1642. The chief task imposed upon him was the compilation of a series of text-books for use in elementary and secondary schools. But progress was slow; the Swedes became impatient, and de Geer grew restive. In consequence, the relations with his patron soon became strained, and continued so during most of the Elbing period. In reply to a complaint from de Geer, Comenius wrote him in September, 1643: "I compose books and do not merely copy those of others. Our proposed work is not merely a book, but a real treasure for the aiding of whose production my patron will assuredly have no cause for regret." He admits that he has been diverted from the completion of a work on language teaching by a philosophic treatise which he considers of far greater importance than the details of methodology.

In addition to the philosophic studies, in which de Geer and the Swedes had little or no interest, Comenius dissipated his energies in other ways. When it became generally known that he had located in Elbing, the wealthy patrons of the local high school petitioned the town council to secure him to give weekly lectures to the pupils. In other ways he identified himself with local interests, which diverted his time from his assigned tasks. Moreover, his connection with the Moravian Brethren compelled him to make frequent trips to Poland to attend ecclesiastical conventions and minister to the needs of the scattered brethren.   De Geer's patience must have been sorely tried, for he sent to Elbing, with annoying frequency, to inquire concerning the progress of the work.   In reply, Comenius begged his patron have patience; he explained the difficult nature of his labors, and assured him that he was making as much progress as was consistent with the nature of his undertaking.

Toward the close of 1646 he went to Sweden and made a personal report to his patron, covering the four years of his employment.   A government committee was appointed to review his work; its report was most favorable to Comenius; and he was urged to get the work in shape for immediate publication.   He had prepared during this time, in spite of distractions, a work on language teaching, which treated of its nature, function, and the laws to be observed in language teaching; a lexicon based on these laws; and a series of graded reading books.

At the death of Justinus, the senior bishop of the Moravian Brethren in 1648, Comenius was elected his successor.   His new duties made his removal to Lissa necessary, and he took with him the unfinished treatises for the Swedes, and sent them to de Geer as rapidly as he was able to complete them.   It caused him no pang of sorrow to sever his connection with the Dutch merchant and the Swedes.   For he was isolated at Elbing; his labors were uncongenial, and the remuneration which he received was small.   It is apparent from his letters, subsequently written, that it was not merely the Dutchman's gold that held him to tasks so arduous and uncongenial.   He hoped by

this connection to secure the moral support of the
Swedes in removing from the Moravian Brethren the
ban which exiled them from their beloved fatherland.

The treaty of Westphalia, however, shattered this
hope.   There was not a single stipulation in favor
of the exiled brethren.   The promises Sweden had
made to Comenius in this matter were disregarded.
In vain he implored Oxenstiern not to forsake his
people.   "My people have aided your arms with their
weapons, the unceasing offerings of their tears and
supplications to God; and now, when they see your
success and may rejoice in the hope for a more favorable issue of affairs, they are troubled with dread
apprehension lest they should be forsaken."   Later he
wrote him: "Of what use is it to us, who are now deprived of every hope of peace, to have assisted you with
our tears in obtaining victory; when, although it lay
within your power to release us from our prison-house,
you surrender us anew into the hands of our oppress-
ors?   Of what avail now all those holy evangelical
alliances formed by our ancestors, and consecrated
with their sacred martyr-blood?"[1]   But these impor-
tunities were of no avail; for, while equal privileges
were granted to the Reformed, Lutheran, and Catholic
churches in Germany, in Bohemia, and Moravia, the
ritual of the latter alone was established.   It was a
severe blow to Comenius, as well as to the whole
brotherhood of the Moravian Church.

The years 1648 to 1650 were passed in ministrations
to the dispersed brethren;[2] he was especially conscien-

[1] The correspondence between Comenius and Oxenstiern over
the treaty of Westphalia is given by Gindely, *Über des Comenius
Leben und Wirksamkeit in der Fremde.*   Vienna, 1855.

[2] For a full account of these labors see Gindely's *Geschichte der
Böhmischen Brüder.*   Prague, 1857–8.

tious in the discharge of the duties of his episcopal office; he established more intimate relations between the Polish and Hungarian branches of the Moravian churches; he sought and secured important financial aid for the brotherhood in England, Holland, and Sweden; he secured positions as teachers for many of his exiled countrymen; and induced the University of Oxford to create stipends for Bohemian students. Gindely remarks that at this period there were few European countries in which the protégés of Comenius could not be found in the capacity of private tutors, public school-teachers, artists, or clergymen.

The impoverished condition of the Moravian Church caused Comenius no little concern, and induced him to look with some favor on the numerous calls to important educational posts which came to him from foreign countries. That from the widow of Prince Rakoczy and her son Sigismund was especially tempting. They wanted him to come to Transylvania, Hungary, and reform the school system. A liberal salary was offered, together with complete facilities for the organization of a school system in accordance with his own views — including a printing establishment for the publication of required books. It was further stipulated that he might bring with him ten or a dozen Bohemian youths to be educated at the expense of the prince and his mother. The scattered members of the Moravian Church in Hungary, in the belief that the presence of the bishop in that country would unify the interests of the brotherhood, also urged him to accept the Transylvanian call, at the same time petitioning the general synod to relieve Comenius of his clerical functions at Lissa for a few years.

The Church granted the petition, and Comenius settled in Saros-Patak, in May, 1650. He at once drew up a sketch of a seven-grade school, which he published a year later under the title *Plan of a pansophic school*. "In scope and breadth of view," remarks a modern historian, "the scheme was centuries in advance of its time, while many of the suggestions which it contained are but imperfectly carried into effect at the present day."

The *Plan* is a detailed course of study with specific directions for the application of the course for the use of teachers. In these directions he explains the great danger of overworking the children; and to avoid this, a rest-pause of a half-hour is provided after each hour's instruction for free, spontaneous play. After each meal a full hour's rest is granted. The pupils are to have eight hours of sleep; they are granted a half-holiday on Sundays and Wednesdays, with fortnight vacations at Christmas, Easter, and Whitsuntide, and a month's vacation in the summer. This gave a school year of forty-two weeks, with thirty hours for school work in each week. The forenoon instruction was as follows: From 6 to 7 o'clock, religious instruction, including hymns, prayers, and Bible readings. From 7.30 to 8.30, theoretical exposition of the new subject-matter of the day's lesson; and from 9 to 10, a practical treatment and review of the same. There was music (and mathematics) in the afternoon from 1 to 2; history from 2.30 to 3.30; and composition, with exercises in style, from 4 to 5.

The *Plan* requires that the seven grades of the school meet in separate rooms, and that a teacher be provided for each grade. In each class, the text-books must be adapted to the capacities of the children. The Vestibulum is the lowest class. Over the door of this room is the motto, "Let no one enter who cannot read." The room is so decorated that the pictures illustrate the subjects taught in this grade; and, by means of these illustrations, the senses are trained. The pupils are taught short maxims containing the most important rules of conduct, a few common Latin words, the elements of arithmetic, the scales in music, and some short hymns and prayers. Writing and drawing are also taught, and special attention is given to the games of the children.

The Janual is the second class. The motto over the class-room door of this grade is, "Let no one enter who is ignorant of mathematics." Provided the more common objects mentioned in the *Janua* cannot be readily obtained, pictures of these objects are hung on the wall. The text-books used are, besides the *Janua*, the Latin vernacular dictionary and the Janual grammar. In composition, the pupils are exercised in the structure of phrases, sentences, and periods; in religion, they learn the catechism; in mathematics, addition and subtraction and plane figures in geometry. There are more advanced exercises in music; and, as in the preceding grade, the teachers are urged to encourage the plays and games of the children.

The Atrial is the third class. Its motto is, "Let no one enter who cannot speak." Here Bible readings, in abridged form and suited to the intelligence of the children, are begun. The text-book is the *Atrium*, together with a grammar of eloquence and a Latin-Latin dictionary. In arithmetic, the pupils master multiplication and division, and in geometry, solid

F

figures. The musical instruction includes harmony
and the rudiments of Latin verse. Famous deeds in
Biblical narrative furnish the basis of the historic
instruction. In composition there are exercises in
style, consisting of paraphrasing and the transposition
of sentences. Before the pupils are permitted to pass
from this grade they must be able to read the Latin
authors readily and to converse in the Latin fluently.

The Philosophical is the fourth class, with the
motto, "Let no one who is ignorant of history enter
here." The walls are decorated with pictures illustrative of arithmetic, geometry, and physics, and connected with this class-room are a chemical laboratory
and a dissecting-room. The religious instruction
includes hymns, Psalms, an epitome of the New Testament, and a life of Christ. The text-book is called
the *Palace of wisdom;* in it the genesis of natural phe-
nomena are described. In mathematics, the pupils
learn the rules of proportion; they begin the study of
trigonometry; also statics, and instruction on musical
instruments. Greek is begun, and the pupils study
natural history through Pliny and Ælian. Comenius
mentions that he does not consider Greek a difficult
study; and he thinks it need cause the pupils no
alarm, since an exhaustive knowledge of Greek is not
required, and the difficulties of the study will be
largely overcome by the use of rational methods of
teaching.

The fifth class is the Logical. Over the door is the
inscription, "Let no one enter who is ignorant of
natural philosophy," and the walls are covered with
the rules of logic. The pupils have a Bible manual
and a class-book on problems in philosophy. The

problems include a survey of things that have been
and may be discovered by man; a formal logic explaining the processes of reasoning, and a repertory of such
philosophical problems as present themselves to the
human mind.   In arithmetic, the rules of partnership
and allegation are studied; in geometry, mensuration
of heights and distances and plane surfaces; in geography, a description of the earth; in astronomy, an
account of the heavens; in history, a survey of
mechanical inventions.   For the formation of a literary style, such historians as Curtius, Cæsar, and Jus-
tin are read.   The study of Greek is continued, and
Isocrates and Plutarch are recommended for reading.
Dramatic performances are introduced in the fifth
class.   Grammar, logic, and metaphysics are represented in conflict, but a reconciliation is finally effected
through study.

The sixth is the Political class.   Its motto, "Let
no one enter who cannot reason."   Sallust, Cicero,
Virgil, and Horace are read for style; provision is
made for verse writing; attention is given to geography and the parts of astronomy dealing with the
planets and the laws of the eclipses; the Bible is read
through; more advanced topics in arithmetic and geometry are taken up; the special class-book studied deals
with human society and the laws of economics; in
Greek the pupils read from Thucydides and Hesiod.
Dramatic performances are continued, the degeneration
and moral downfall of Solomon being rendered.

The seventh and last grade of the course is the
Philosophic.   Its motto is, "Let no one enter who
is irreligious."   The instruction is of an essentially
theological character.   On the walls are inscribed

numerous mystic symbols illustrative of the hidden wisdom of the Holy Scriptures. The most devotional Psalms and church hymns are used in the school exercises. There are readings from the Scriptures, the works of the most inspired theologians and martyrs, and a *résumé* of Christian beliefs, duties, and aspirations, all written in the phraseology of the Bible. The text-book of the grade is ultra-religious in character. It includes (1) an account of the earthly and heavenly revelations of God; (2) a commentary for Scriptural reading; and (3) a detailed account of the mysteries of salvation. In arithmetic, the sacred and mystic numbers that occur in the Scriptures; in architecture, the sacred structures as exemplified by Noah's ark, the tabernacle, and the Temple; in history, the general history of the Church; and in ancient language, Hebrew takes the place of Greek — this, that the students may be able to read and understand the Scriptures in the original text. Oratory is studied that those who become preachers may know how to address a congregation, and that those who engage in politics may know how to reason with their hearers.

Such is a condensed survey of the course of study which Comenius devised for the schools at Saros-Patak; and in no small degree his reputation as a reformer rests upon this piece of work. For the Saros-Patak *Plan* became a model for educators in many lands, and the progenitor of a long line of graded schemes of instruction which constitute such an essential feature of the educational economy of to-day. Not only were subjects of study graded in accordance with the laws of the development of child-mind, but text-books were graded as well. Moreover, the scheme made necessary the employment of teachers who comprehended the character of the work, and, more particularly, those with some appreciation of the natural history of the child and the causes which condition its growth. Little as Comenius understood psychology, at least in the modern use of that term, he was alive to the fact that in childhood the senses are keenest, and that the line of least resistance in the acquisition of new impressions is through (1) objects, (2) pictures, and (3) interesting verbal descriptions in the mother-tongue.

His labors at Saros-Patak terminated at the close of the fourth year, during which time the first three grades of the *Plan* were organized. All contemporary evidence confirms the success of the scheme. Although so marked a departure from traditional educational practices, it succeeded to a degree that must have been surprising even to Comenius himself. The fact that the teachers in the schools were trained under Comenius at Lissa did much, doubtless, to remove otherwise possible frictions.

But careful gradation was not the only marked reform carried out at Saros-Patak during this period. Pictures were introduced as aids in teaching, and the first child's picture book, the first of a long line of books so popular in our own day, was written. This was the famous *Orbis pictus*, to be discussed in a subsequent chapter.

Comenius returned to Lissa in 1654, to resume his ecclesiastical labors. But his sojourn was brief; for, with the invasion of Poland by the Swedes, came the fall and conflagration of the city. Comenius escaped, "almost in a state of nudity," to use his own words.

He had not only lost his property and his library in the conflagration, but he had sustained a yet greater loss in the burning of his numerous manuscripts, and, more important (to him) than all the others, his entire pansophic work, on the composition of which he had labored so arduously for many years. Writing to Montanus, he says, "The loss of this work I shall cease to lament only when I cease to breathe." He escaped from Lissa to Silesia, where he found refuge for a time in the home of a nobleman. He shortly afterward pushed on to Frankfort, but not feeling secure here he moved to Hamburg, where for two months he was prostrated by a severe illness.

CHAPTER V

Flight to Amsterdam — Reception by Lawrence de Geer — Religious freedom in Holland — Publication of the complete edition of his writings — Other educational activities — The " One thing needful " — Death at Amsterdam and burial at Naärden — Family history of Comenius — Alleged call to the presidency of Harvard College — Portraits — Personal characteristics.

DURING his last year's residence at Saros-Patak, Comenius had sustained a great loss in the death of his friend and former patron, Lewis de Geer. In a funeral oration which he composed, he characterized his benefactor as "a man pious toward God, just toward men, merciful to the distressed, and meritoriously great and illustrious among all men." The rich Dutch merchant bequeathed his estates to his son, Lawrence de Geer of Amsterdam; and not only his estates, but also his deep interest in the welfare of the Moravian reformer.

Learning of the severe illness of Comenius, Lawrence de Geer wrote him to leave Hamburg and come directly to Amsterdam, where all the needs of his closing years would be provided. The younger de Geer, it would seem, had not only a real and profound affection for the aged Comenius, but also a keen and intelligent interest in all his schemes for educational reform.

Amsterdam proved, indeed, a haven of rest to the weary wanderer. At this time the city enjoyed greater religious freedom than perhaps any other city in Europe. Says Benham: "Comenius found himself in the midst of a community then enjoying the largest amount of religious toleration to be found anywhere in Europe, and with it a great diversity of religious opinions. Unitarians expelled from their own countries here united themselves to the friends of speculative philosophy among the Remonstrants and Arminians; and the philosophy of Descartes here found admirers even among the members of the Reformed Church. The truly evangelical Comenius had become known to many through his writings, which, together with the influence of his patron's son, Lawrence de Geer, who continued his father's benevolence, induced rich merchants to intrust him with the education of their sons; so that, with the additions accruing from his literary labors, Comenius found a supply of food and raiment, and was thereby content."

In spite of his advanced age, these closing years of his life at Amsterdam were busy ones; for besides ministering to the needs of the scattered and disheartened ecclesiastics of the Moravian Brethren, he engaged somewhat in private teaching, and saw through the press a complete edition of his educational writings. It was a magnificent volume of more than a thousand pages, and was printed by Christopher Cunard and Gabriel à Roy under the title *All the didactical works of J. A. Comenius.*

The publication of this handsome folio, containing all his educational writings, was made possible by the generosity of Lawrence de Geer. The first part of the folio, written between 1627 and 1642, contains (1) a brief narration of the circumstances which led the author to write these studies; (2) the *Great didactic*, showing the method of teaching all things; (3) the *School of infancy*, being an essay on the education of youth during the first six years; (4) an account of a six-class vernacular school; (5) the *Janua;* (6) the *Vestibulum;* (7) David Vechner's *Model of a temple of Latinity;* (8) a didactic dissertation on the quadripartite study of the Latin language; (9) the circle of all the sciences; (10) various criticisms on the same; (11) explanations of attempts at pansophy.

The second part of the folio, written between 1642 and 1650, contains (1) new reasons for continuing to devote attention to didactic studies; (2) new methods of studying languages, built upon didactic foundations; (3) vestibule of the Latin language adapted to the laws of the most recent methods of language teaching; (4) new gate of the Latin language exhibiting the structure of things and words in their natural order; (5) a Latin and German introductory lexicon explaining a multitude of derived words; (6) a grammar of the Latin and vernacular, with short commentaries; (7) treatise on the Latin language of the *Atrium;* (8) certain opinions of the learned on these new views of language teaching.

The third part of the work, written between 1650 and 1654, contains (1) a brief account of his call to Hungary; (2) a sketch of the seven-class pansophic school; (3) an oration on the culture of innate capacities; (4) an oration on books as the primary instruments in the cultivation of innate capacities; (5) on the obstacles to the acquisition of encyclopædic culture and some means of removing these obstacles; (6) a short and pleasant way of learning to read and understand the Latin authors; (7) on scholastic erudition; (8) on driving idleness from the schools; (9) laws for a well-regulated school; (10) the *Orbis pictus;* (11) on scholastic play; (12) valedictory oration delivered on the occasion of the completion of his labors at Saros-Patak; (13) funeral oration on the life and character of Lewis de Geer.

The fourth part of the work represents the years from 1654 to 1657. It contains (1) an account of the author's didactic studies; (2) a little boy to little boys, or all things to all; (3) apology for the Latinity of Comenius; (4) the art of wisely reviewing one's own opinions; (5) exits from scholastic labyrinths into the open plain; (6) the formation of a Latin college; (7) the living printing-press, or the art of impressing wisdom compendiously, copiously, and elegantly, not on paper, but on the mind; (8) the best condition of the mind; (9) a devout commendation of the study of wisdom.

In addition to his literary labors, he gave much time to the administration of church affairs; for Lissa had risen from her ashes and was more prosperous than before the war. Here congregated again many adherents of the Moravian brotherhood, and the college was rebuilt and resumed its beneficent pedagogic influence. From this centre the Moravian influence spread anew to many parts of Europe. England, Prussia, and other Protestant countries were generous in their contributions toward the restoration of Moravian churches. All this money was sent to Comenius at Amsterdam, and by him apportioned to the scattered brethren. He received thirty thousand dollars from England alone during the years 1658 and 1659;

the only stipulation made in the disposition of the money was that a portion of it should be used for the printing of Polish and Bohemian Bibles. The last years of his life were occupied almost wholly in such ministrations.

He published in 1668 his swan song, the *One thing needful*. This is his farewell address to the world. It delineates in a forceful yet modest way his aspirations for educational reform, gives expression of the deep faith which sustained him during the long years of his weary pilgrimage, and burns with enthusiastic zeal for the welfare of mankind — the burning passion of his life. He was well prepared at the advanced age of seventy-six years to sum up the experience of a long and afflicted life.

A few citations from this touching bit of reminiscence will hint at the motives which actuated him in his life-work as an educational reformer. "I thank God that I have been all my life a man of aspirations; and although He has brought me into many labyrinths, yet He has so protected me that either I have soon worked my way out of them, or He has brought me by His own hand to the enjoyment of holy rest. For the desire after good, if it is always in the heart, is a living stream that flows from God, the fountain of all good. The blame is ours if we do not follow the stream to its source or to its overflow into the sea, where there is fulness and satiety of good."

"One of my chief employments has been the improvement of schools, which I undertook and continued for many years from the desire to deliver the youth in the schools from the labyrinth in which they are entangled. Some have held this business foreign to a theologian, as if Christ had not connected together and given to his beloved disciple Peter at the same time the two commands, 'Feed my sheep' and 'Feed my lambs.' I thank Christ for inspiring me with such affection toward his lambs, and for regulating my exertions in the form of educational works. I trust that when the winter of indifference has passed that my endeavors will bring forth some fruit."

"My life here was not my native country, but a pilgrimage; my home was ever changing, and I found nowhere an abiding resting place. But now I see my heavenly country near at hand, to whose gates my Saviour has gone before me to prepare the way. After years of wandering and straying from the direction of my journey, delayed by a thousand extraneous diversions, I am at last within the bounds of the promised land."

The rest and peace and glory which he so hopefully anticipated came to him at Amsterdam on the 15th of November, in the year 1670. His remains were conveyed to Naärden, a small town on the Zuyder Zee, twelve miles east of Amsterdam, where they were interred in the French Reformed Church, on the 22d of November. The figure 8 was the only epitaph placed on his tomb. More than a century afterward the church was transformed into a military barracks, and for many years the date of his death, the church in which he was buried, and the grave inclosing his remains were unknown. But in 1871 Mr. de Röper, a lawyer residing in Naärden, found among his father's papers the church register, the sexton's account book, and other documents relating to the old French Reformed Church. After the figure 8, in the church

register, was this entry: "John Amos Comenius, the
famous author of the *Janua Linguarum;* interred the
22d of November, 1670." A diligent search was
instituted, and the grave was found. An aged woman
residing in Naärden recalled the location of the French
Reformed Church as the present site of the barracks.
By permission of the commanding officer, an examination was made and the tombstone marked 8 was found.
The remains were subsequently removed to a little
park in Naärden, where there was erected to his
memory, in 1892, by friends of education in Europe
and America, a handsome monument. This consists
of a pyramid of rough stones with two white marble
slabs containing gold-furrowed inscriptions in Latin,
Dutch, and Czech (Bohemian): "A grateful posterity
to the memory of John Amos Comenius, born at
Nivnitz on the 28th of March, 1592; died at Amsterdam on the 15th of November, 1670; buried at Naärden on the 22d of November, 1670. He fought a
good fight." A room in the town hall at Naärden has
been set aside as a permanent Comenius museum,
where will be found a collection of his portraits, sets
of the different editions of his writings, and the old
stone slab containing the figure 8.

The present work being an educational rather than
a personal life of Comenius, no reference has thus far
been made to his family life. It may be noted briefly
that he married, in 1624, Elizabeth Cyrrill, with
whom he had five children, a son (Daniel) and four
daughters. Elizabeth died in 1648 and he married
again on the 17th of May, 1649, Elizabeth Gainsowa,
with whom he appears to have had no children. A
third marriage is mentioned by some of his biog-

raphers, but the statement lacks corroboration.   One
daughter, Elizabeth, married Peter Figulus Jablonsky,
who was bishop of the Church from November, 1662,
until his death, January the 12th, 1670.   Their son
Daniel Ernst Jablonsky was consecrated a bishop of
the Polish branch of the Moravian Church at Lissa
March the 10th, 1699.   He served the Church until
his death, May the 25th, 1741.

An account of the life of Comenius would be incomplete without some reference to his alleged call to
the presidency of Harvard College.   This rests upon
an unconfirmed statement by Cotton Mather.   In his
Magnalia[1] he says: "Mr. Henry Dunster continued
the Praesident of Harvard-College until his unhappy
Entanglement in the Snares of Anabaptism fill'd the
Overseers with uneasie Fears, lest the Students by his
means should come to be Ensnared: Which Uneasi-
ness was at length so signified unto him, that on
October 24, 1654, he presented unto the Overseers,
an Instrument under his Hands, wherein he Resigned
his Presidentship and they accepted his Resignation.
That brave Old Man Johannes Amos Commenius, the
Fame of whose Worth has been Trumpetted as far as
more than Three Languages (whereof every one is
Endebted unto his *Janua*) could carry it, was agreed
withall, by our Mr. Winthrop in his Travels through
the Low Countries to come over into New England
and Illuminate this College and Country in the Quality
of a President.   But the Solicitations of the Swedish

---

[1] *Magnalia Christi Americana, or the ecclesiastical history of
New England.*   By the Reverend and Learned Cotton Mather and
Pastor of the North Church in Boston, New England.   London, 1702.
Book IV, p. 128.

Ambassador, diverting him another way, that Incomparable Moravian became not an American."

The following evidence makes improbable this call: —

1. Some years ago the writer asked Professor Paul H. Hanus to ascertain for him if the records of Harvard College corroborated Mather's statement. After examining the proceedings of the overseers and all other records of the college during its early history, he reported that he could not find the slightest corroboration of Mather's statement, and that he seriously doubted its accuracy.

2. The historians of the college — Peirce, Quincy, and Eliot — do not allude to the matter. And President Josiah Quincy,[1] in his complete and standard history of the institution, refers to the "loose and exaggerated terms in which Mather and Johnson, and other writers of that period, speak of the early donations to the college, and the obscurity, and not to say confusion, in which they appear in the first records of the seminary."

3. Careful examination has been made of the numerous lives of Comenius printed in the German language, as well as those printed in the Czech; and, although less noteworthy distinctions are recorded, there is no mention of a call to Harvard College or America.

4. In the *Journals* of Governor John Winthrop of Massachusetts, there are no allusions to Comenius. Governor Winthrop died in 1649; and it was not until 1653 that President Dunster fell "into the briers of

[1] *The history of Harvard university.* By Josiah Quincy. Boston, 1840. 2 vols.

Antpædo-baptism," when he bore "public testimony
in the church at Cambridge against the administration
of baptism to any infant whatsoever." And the historians of the college report that up to this time
(1653) Dunster's administration had been singularly
satisfactory, so that there could have been no thought
of providing his successor before the death of Governor
Winthrop. Mather is either in error or he does not
refer to Governor Winthrop of Massachusetts. He
may refer to Governor Winthrop of Connecticut,
the eldest son of the Massachusetts governor, although
evidence is wanting to show that the Connecticut
governor had anything to do with the management of
Harvard College. Young Winthrop was in England
from August the 3d, 1641, until the early part of 1643.
It will be recalled that Comenius spent the winter of
1641–1642 in London, and the fact that both knew
Hartlib most intimately would suggest that they must
have met. In a letter which Hartlib wrote to Winthrop
after the latter's return to America, he says, "Mr.
Comenius is continually diverted by particular con-
troversies of Socinians and others from his main
Pansophical Worke." [1]

5. Mather is clearly in error in regard to the date
of the call of Comenius to Sweden. The negotiations
were begun in 1641 and were completed in August of
the next year, so that the "solicitations of the Swedish Ambassador diverting him another way" took
place more than twelve years before the beginning of

---

[1] *Correspondence of Hartlib, Haak, Oldenburg, and others of the
founders of the Royal Society with Governor Winthrop of Connecticut*, 1661–1672. With an introduction and notes by Robert C. Winthrop. Boston, 1878.

the troubles at Cambridge which led to the resignation of Dunster.

With so many flaws in Mather's statement, and the absence of corroborative evidence, it seems altogether improbable that Comenius was ever called to the presidency of Harvard College.[1]

In closing, brief mention may be made of his most dominant physical and personal characteristics. Several excellent portraits of Comenius are in existence, the best perhaps being by Hollar and Glover. From these it is apparent that he was a man of imposing figure, with high forehead, long chin, and soft, pathetic eyes. It is not difficult to read into his sad, expressive countenance the force of the expression in his last published utterance, "My whole life was merely the visit of a guest; I had no fatherland."

There is no conflicting evidence on the personal life of the reformer; but rather unanimous agreement on the sweetness and beauty of his character. Says Palacky: "In his intercourse with others, Comenius was in an extraordinary degree friendly, conciliatory, and humble; always ready to serve his neighbor and sacrifice himself. His writings, as well as his walk and conversation, show the depth of his feeling, his goodness, his uprightness, and his fear of God. He never cast back upon his opponents what they meted out to him. He never condemned, no matter how

[1] For further discussion of the question see my article, "Was Comenius called to the presidency of Harvard?" in the *Educational Review*, November, 1896, Vol. XII, pp. 378–382, and the article by Mr. James H. Blodgett in the same Review for November, 1898, Vol. XVI, pp. 390–393; also the closing chapter in Professor Hanus' *Educational aims and educational values* (New York, 1899), pp. 206–211.

G

great the injustice which he was made to suffer. At
all times, with fullest resignation, whether joy or
sorrow was his portion, he honored and praised the
Lord." Raumer says of him: "Comenius is a grand
and venerable figure of sorrow. Wandering, perse-
cuted, and homeless during the terrible and desolating
Thirty Years' War, he never despaired, but, with
enduring and faithful truth, labored unceasingly to
prepare youth by a better education for a better future.
His unfailing aspirations lifted up in a large part of
Europe many good men prostrated by the terrors of
the times and inspired them with the hope that by
pious and wise systems of education there might be
reared up a race of men more pleasing to God." Well
might Herder say: "Comenius was a noble priest of
humanity, whose single end and aim in life was the
welfare of all mankind."

CHAPTER VI

PHILOSOPHY OF EDUCATION

The *Great didactic* — Conditions under which produced — Aim of
the book. Purpose of education — Man's craving for knowledge
— Youth the time for training — Private instruction undesirable
— Education for girls as well as boys — Uniform methods. Education according to nature — How nature teaches — Selection and
adaptation of materials — Organization of pupils into classes —
Correlation of studies. Methods of instruction — Science — Arts
— Language — Morals — Religion. Types of educational institutions — The mother's school — School of the mother-tongue —
Latin school — University. School discipline — Character and
purpose of discipline — Corporal punishment only in cases of
moral perversity.

The Great Didactic

MOST comprehensive of all of the educational writings of Comenius is the *Great didactic*. It was
planned in 1628, while yet in the full possession of
his vigor, before misfortune had hampered his usefulness and persecution had made him a wanderer.
Written originally in the Czech, it was translated into
the Latin and published at Amsterdam in 1657. The
original Czech manuscript was discovered at Lissa in
1841, and presented to the museum at Prague; but
the Austrian censors of the press forbade its publication because Comenius was a Bohemian exile (!).
Through the exertions of the museum authorities, however, it was allowed to be printed in 1849. Professor
Laurie gave English readers a summary of the *Great*

didactic in his *Life and educational works of John Amos Comenius* (London, 1883); but the first complete translation was made by Mr. M. W. Keatinge of Edinburgh in 1896.

The full title is: *The great didactic setting forth the whole art of teaching all things to all men ; or a certain inducement to found such schools in all parishes, towns, and villages of every Christian kingdom that the entire youth of both sexes, none being excepted, shall quickly, pleasantly, and thoroughly become learned in the sciences, pure in morals, trained in piety, and in this manner instructed in all things necessary for the present and future life, in which, with respect to everything that is suggested, its fundamental principles are set forth from the essential nature of the matter, its truth is proved by examples, from the several mechanical arts its order is clearly set forth in years, months, days, and hours ; and finally an easy and sure method is shown by which it can be pleasantly brought into existence.*

The purpose of the *Great didactic*, as announced by Comenius in the preface, is to seek and find a method of instruction by which teachers may teach less, but learners may learn more; schools may be the scene of less noise, aversion, and useless labor, but of more leisure, enjoyment, and solid progress; the Christian community have less darkness, perplexity, and dissension, but more light, peace, and rest. He promises in his "greeting" an "art of teaching all things to all men, and of teaching them with certainty, so that the result cannot fail." Among the uses of such an art he notes the advantage (1) to parents, that they may know that if correct methods have been employed with unerring accuracy, it is impossible that the is iniquitous, and should be promptly corrected; but an offence against Priscian is a stain that may be wiped out by the sponge of blame. In a word, the object of discipline should be to stir the pupils to revere God, to assist their fellows, and to perform the labors and duties of life with alacrity.

structure, one part depends upon another through the harmony and perfection of the movements — so it is with man. All this harmony and perfection is made possible through education.

He gave no bad definition, remarks Comenius, who said that man was a "teachable animal." But he must be taught, since he is born only with aptitudes. Before he can sit, stand, walk, or use his hands, he requires instruction. It is the law of all created things that they develop gradually and ultimately reach a state of perfection. Plato was right when he said, "If properly educated, man is the gentlest and most divine of created beings; but if left uneducated or subjected to a false training, he is the most intractable thing in the world."

Education is necessary for all classes of society; and this is the more apparent when we consider the marked individual differences to be found among human beings. No one doubts that the stupid need instruction that they may outgrow their stupidity. But clever and precocious minds require more careful instruction than dull and backward minds; since those who are mentally active, if not occupied with useful things, will busy themselves with what is useless, curious, and pernicious. Just as a millstone grinds itself away with noise if wheat is not supplied, so an active mind, if void of serious things, entangles itself with vain, curious, and noxious thoughts, and becomes the cause of its own destruction.

The time for education is in early youth.[1] God has,

[1] For an excellent discussion of the meaning of infancy see Professor John Fiske's *Excursions of an evolutionist* (Boston, 1896), pp. 306–319, and Professor Nicholas Murray Butler's *Meaning of education* (New York, 1898), pp. 3–34.

accordingly, made the years of childhood unsuitable for anything but education; and this matter was interposed by the deliberate intent of a wise Providence. Youth is a period of great plasticity. It is in the nature of everything that comes into being to bend and form easily while tender; but when the plastic period has passed to alter only with great difficulty. If one wishes to become a good tailor, writer, or musician, he must apply himself to his art from his earliest youth, during the period when his imagination is most active and when his fingers are most flexible. Only during the years of childhood is it possible to train the muscles to do skilled work. If, then, parents have the welfare of their children at heart, and if the good of the human race be dear to the civil and ecclesiastical guardians of society, let them hasten to make provision for the timely planting, pruning, and watering of the plants of heaven that these may be prudently formed in letters, virtue, and piety.

Private education is not desirable. Children should be trained in common, since better results and more pleasures are to be obtained when they are taught together in classes. Not only is class teaching a saving of labor over private instruction, but it introduces a rivalry that is both needful and helpful. Moreover, young children learn much that is useful by imitation through association with school-fellows. Comenius, it may be remarked, was one of the first of the educational reformers to see clearly the value of class teaching and graded instruction. His reforms in this direction have already been noted.

School training is necessary for the children of all

grades of society, not of the rich and powerful only, but the poor and lowly as well. Let none be neglected, unless God has denied him sense and intelligence. When it is urged that the laboring classes need no school education, let it be also recalled that they are expected to think, obey, and do good.

Girls should be educated as well as boys. No satisfactory reason can be given why women should be excluded from the pursuits of knowledge, whether in the Latin or in the mother-tongue. They are formed in the image of God as well as men; and they are endowed with equal sharpness of mind and capacity for learning, often, indeed, with more than the opposite sex. Why, then, should we admit them to the alphabet, and afterwards drive them away from books? Comenius takes issue with most writers on education that study will make women blue-stockings and chatterboxes. On the contrary, he maintains, the more their minds are occupied with the fruits of learning, the less room and temptation there will be for gossip and folly.

Not only should education be common to all classes of society, but the subjects of instruction should be common to the whole range of knowledge. Comenius holds that it is the business of educators to take strong and vigorous measures that no man in his journey through life may encounter anything so unknown to him that he will be unable to pass sound judgment upon it and turn it to its proper use without serious error. This desire for encyclopædic learning, as already noted, dominated his life and writings.

But even Comenius recognized the futility of thoroughness in a wide range of instruction, and he expresses willingness to be satisfied if men know the principles, the causes, and the uses of all things in existence. It is general culture — something about a great many things — that he demands.

Comenius clearly saw that the conditions of educational institutions were wholly inadequate for the realization of these purposes — (1) because of an insufficient number of schools, and (2) because of the unscientific character of current methods of instruction. The exhortations of Martin Luther, he observes, remedied the former shortcoming, but it remains for the future to improve the latter.

The best intellects are ruined by unsympathetic and unpedagogic methods. Such great severity characterizes the schools that they are looked upon as terrors for the boys and shambles for their intellects. Most of the students contract a dislike for learning, and many leave school altogether. The few who are forced by parents and guardians to remain acquire a most preposterous and wretched sort of education, so that instead of tractable lambs, the schools produce wild asses and restive mules. Nothing could be more wretched than the discipline of the schools. "What should be gently instilled into the intellect is violently impressed upon it, nay, rather flogged into it. How many, indeed, leave the schools and universities with scarcely a notion of true learning." Comenius laments that he and many thousands of his contemporaries have miserably lost the sweet springtime of life and wasted the fresh years of youth on scholastic trifles.

Education according to Nature

Comenius proposes to so reconstruct systems of education that (1) all shall be educated, except those to whom God has denied understanding, in all those subjects calculated to make men wise, virtuous, and pious; (2) the course of training, being a preparation for life, shall be completed before maturity is attained; (3) and schools shall be conducted without blows, gently and pleasantly, in the most natural manner. Bold innovator! How clearly he perceived the faults of the schools of his day; with what keen insight he formulated methods for their improvement; and with what hope in the reform which has gone forward steadily for these two hundred and seventy-five years, but which even now is far from being an accomplished fact!

The basis of the reform which he advocates is an application of the principle of order — order in the management of time, in the arrangement of subjects taught, and in the methods employed. Nature furnishes us a criterion for order in all matters pertaining to the improvement of human society. Certain universal principles, which are fundamental to his philosophy of education, are deduced from nature. These, stripped of their tedious examples and details, are: —

1. Nature observes a suitable time.

2. She prepares the material before she attempts to give it form.

3. She chooses a fit subject to act upon, or first submits her subject to a suitable treatment in order to make it fit.

4. She is not confused in her operations; but, in her onward march, advances with precision from one point to another.

5. In all the operations of nature, development is from within.

6. In her formative processes, she begins with the universal and ends with the particular.

7. Nature makes no leaps, but proceeds step by step.

8. When she begins a thing, she does not leave off until the operation is completed.

9. She avoids all obstacles that are likely to interfere with her operations.

With nature as our guide, Comenius believes that the process of education will be easy, (1) if it is begun before the mind is corrupted; (2) if the mind is prepared to receive it; (3) if we proceed from the general to the particular, from what is easy to what is more complex; (4) if the pupils are not overburdened with too many different studies; (5) if the instruction is graded to the stages of the mental development of the learners; (6) if the interests of the children are consulted and their intellects are not forced along lines for which they have no natural bent; (7) if everything is taught through the medium of the senses; (8) if the utility of instruction is emphasized; and (9) if everything is taught by one and the same method.

Nature begins by a careful selection of materials, therefore education should commence early; the pupils should not have more than one teacher in each subject, and before anything else is done, the morals should be rendered harmonious by the teacher's influence.

Nature always makes preparation for each advance

step; therefore, the desire to know and to learn should be excited in children in every way possible, and the method of instruction should lighten the drudgery, that there may be nothing to hinder progress in school studies.

Nature develops everything from beginnings which, though insignificant in appearance, possess great potential strength; whereas, the practice of most teachers is in direct opposition to this principle. Instead of starting with fundamental facts, they begin with a chaos of diverse conclusions.

Nature advances from what is easy to what is more difficult. It is, therefore, wrong to teach the unknown through the medium of that which is equally unknown. Such errors may be avoided if pupils and teachers talk in the same language and explanations are given in the language that the pupil understands; if grammars and dictionaries are adapted in the language and to the understanding of the pupils; if, in the study of a foreign language, the pupils first learn to understand it, then to write it, and lastly to speak it; if in such study the pupils get to know first that which is nearest to their mental vision, then that which lies moderately near, then that which is more remote, and lastly that which is farthest off; and if children be made to exercise first their senses, then their memory, and finally their understanding.

Nature does not overburden herself, but is content with a little at a time; therefore the mental energies of the pupils should not be dissipated over a wide range of subject-matter.

Nature advances slowly; therefore school sessions should be shortened to four hours; pupils should be forced to memorize as little as possible; school instruction should be graded to the ages and capacities of the children.

Nature compels nothing to advance that is not driven forward by its own mature strength; therefore it follows that nothing should be taught to children not demanded by their age, interests, and mental ability.

Nature assists her operations in every possible manner; therefore children should not be punished for inability to learn. Rather, instruction should be given through the senses that it may be retained in the memory with less effort.

Nothing is produced by nature the practical application of which is not evident; therefore those things only should be taught whose application can be easily demonstrated.

Nature is uniform in all her operations; hence the same method of instruction should be adapted to all subjects of study, and the text-books in each subject should, as far as possible, be of the same editions.

Comenius observes that there is a very general complaint that few leave school with a thorough education, and that most of the instruction retained in after life is little more than a mere shadow of true knowledge. He considers that the complaint is well corroborated by facts, and attributes the cause to the insignificant and unimportant studies with which the schools occupy themselves. If we would correct this evil, we must go to the school of nature and investigate the methods she adopts to give endurance to the beings which she has created.

A method should be found by means of which each person will be able not only to bring into his mental consciousness that which he has learned, but at the same time to pass sound judgment on the objective facts to which his information refers. This will be possible if only those subjects are studied which will be of real service in the later life; if such subjects be taught without digression or interruption; if a thorough grounding precede the detailed instruction; if all that comes later be based upon what has gone before; if great stress be laid on the points of resemblance between cognate subjects; if the studies be arranged with reference to the pupils' present mental development, and if knowledge be fixed in the memory by constant use.

In support of his principle of thoroughness, Comenius adduces the following proofs from nature: Nothing is produced by nature that is useless. When she forms a body, she omits nothing that is necessary. She does not operate on anything unless it possesses foundations, and she strikes her roots deep and develops everything from them. She never remains at rest, but advances continually; never begins anything fresh at the expense of work already begun, but proceeds with what she has started and brings it to completion. She knits everything together in continuous combination, preserving due proportion with respect to both quality and quantity. Through constant exercise she becomes strong and fruitful.

Progress is less a question of strength than of skill. Hitherto little has been accomplished in the school-life of the child, because no set landmarks have been set up as goals to be reached by the pupils; things naturally associated are not taught together; the arts and sciences are scarcely ever thought of as an encyclopædic whole; the methods employed are as numerous and diverse as the schools and teachers; instruction is individual and private, and not public and general, and books are selected with too little regard for the value of their contents. If these matters could be reformed, there is no doubt in the mind of Comenius that the whole circle of the sciences might be covered during the period of school training. Toward the solution of this problem he answers the following questions: —

1. How can a single teacher instruct a large number of children at the same time? In answer, he maintains that it is not only possible for one teacher to instruct several hundred children (!) at once, but that it is essential for the best interests of both the teacher and the children (!!). The larger the number of pupils, the greater will be the teacher's interest in his work; and the keener his interest, the greater the enthusiasm of his pupils. In the same way, to the children, the presence of a number of companions will be productive not only of utility, but also of enjoyment, since they will mutually stimulate and assist one another. For children of this age, emulation and rivalry are the best incentives to study. The reader will observe that this scheme of Comenius contemplates some adaptation of the system of pupil teaching, and that it interdicts all efforts at individual instruction.

2. How far is it possible for pupils to be taught from the same book? It is an undisputed fact, says Comenius, that too many facts presented to the mind at the same time distract the attention. It will, therefore, be of great advantage if the pupils be permitted to use no books except those which have been expressly

composed for the class in which they are. Such books should contain a complete, thorough, and accurate epitome of all the subjects of instruction. They should give a true representation of the entire universe; should be written simply and clearly — preferably in the form of a dialogue; and should give the pupils sufficient assistance to enable them, if necessary, to pursue their studies without the help of a master.

3. How is it possible for all the pupils in a school to do the same thing at one time? This may be accomplished by having a course of instruction commence at a definite time of each year; and by and by so dividing the course of instruction that each year, each month, each week, each day, each hour may have a definite appointed task for it.

4. How is it possible to teach everything according to one and the same method? That there is only one natural method has already been satisfactorily demonstrated (to the mind of Comenius), and the universal adoption of this natural method will be as great a boon to pupils as a plain and undeviating road is to travellers.

5. How can many things be explained in a few words? The purpose of education is not to fill the mind with a dreary waste of words from books. Rightly says Seneca of instruction: "Its administration should resemble the sowing of seed, in which stress is laid not on the quantity, but on the quality."

6. How is it possible to do two or three things by a single operation? It may be laid down as a general rule that each subject should be taught in combination with those which are correlative to it. Reading, penmanship, spelling, language, and nature study should

work together in the acquisition and expression of ideas. As Professor Hanus[1] has pointed out, Comenius clearly foreshadowed the correlation and coördination of school studies at least two centuries before Herbart. Indeed, he went so far as to urge the correlation of school instruction with the plays and games of children. He urged that children be given tools and allowed to imitate the different handicrafts, by playing at farming, at politics, at being soldiers or architects. In the game of war they may be allowed to take the part of field-marshals, generals, captains, and standard-bearers. In that of politics they may be kings, ministers, chancellors, secretaries, and ambassadors, as well as senators, consuls, and lawyers; since such pleasantries often lead to serious things. Thus, maintains Comenius, would be fulfilled Luther's wish that the studies of the young at school might be so organized that the pupils would take as much pleasure in them as playing at ball all day. In this way, the schools might become a real prelude to the more serious duties of practical life.

Methods of Instruction

A correct method of instruction was to Comenius, as has already been pointed out, the panacea for most of the ills of teaching. He made reform in methodology the starting point of all his schemes for educational improvement. In the *Great didactic* he considers reform in methods of instructing in the sciences, arts, language, morals, and religion.

[1] Permanent influence of Comenius, *Educational Review*, March, 1892. Vol. III, pp. 226-236.

H

1. *Science.* Knowledge of nature or science requires objects to be perceived and sufficient attention for the perception of the objects. The youth who would comprehend the sciences must observe four rules: (1) he must keep the eye of his mind pure; (2) he must see that the proper relationship is established between the eye and the object; (3) he must attend to the object; (4) he must proceed from one object to another in accordance with a suitable method.

The beginning of wisdom in the sciences consists, not in the mere learning of the names of things, but in the actual perception of the things themselves. It is after the thing has been grasped by the senses that language should fulfil its function of still further explaining it. The senses are the trusty servants of the memory, leading to the permanent retention of the knowledge that has been acquired. Reasoning, also, is conditioned and mediated by the experience gained through sense-perception. It is evident, therefore, that if we wish to develop a true love and knowledge of science, we must take special care to see that everything is learned by actual observation through sense-perception. This should be the golden rule of teachers: Everything should as far as possible be placed before the senses.

When the objects themselves cannot be procured, representations of them may be used; models may be constructed or the objects may be represented by means of engravings. This is especially needful in such studies as geography, geometry, botany, zoölogy, physiology, and physics. It requires both labor and expense to produce models, but the results of such aids will more than repay the efforts. In the absence of both objects and models, the things may be represented by means of pictures.[1]

2. *Arts.* "Theory," says Vives, "is easy and short, but has no result other than the gratification that it affords. Practice, on the other hand, is difficult and prolix, but of immense utility." Since this is so, remarks Comenius, we should diligently seek out a method by which the young may be easily led to the application of such natural forces as one finds in the arts.

In the acquisition of an art, three things are required : (1) a model which the pupil may examine and then try to imitate; (2) material on which the new form is to be impressed; and (3) instruments by the aid of which the work is accomplished. After these have been provided, three things more are necessary before an art can be learned — a proper use of the materials, skilled guidance, and frequent practice.

Progress in the art studies is primarily through practice. Let the pupils learn to write by writing, to talk by talking, and to sing by singing. Since imitation is such an important factor in the mastery of an art, it is sheer cruelty to try to force a pupil to do that which you wish done, while the pupil is ignorant of your wishes. The use of instruments should be shown in practice, and not by words; by example, rather than by precept. It is many years since Quintilian wrote, " Through precepts the way is long and difficult, while through examples it is short and practicable." But alas! remarks Comenius, how little heed the schools pay to this advice. Man is essentially an imitative

[1] The *Orbis pictus*, the first child's picture-book, was subsequently prepared to meet this need.

animal, and it is by imitation that children learn to walk, to run, to talk, and to play.[1] Rules are like thorns to the understanding, since to grasp them requires a degree of mental development not common during the elementary school life of the child.

Comenius would have the first attempts at imitation as accurate as possible, since whatever comes first is the foundation of that which is to follow. All haste in the first steps should be avoided, lest we proceed to the advanced work before the elements have been mastered.

Perfect instruction in the arts is based on both synthesis and analysis. The synthetic steps should generally come first, since we should commence with what is easy, and our own efforts are always easiest to understand. But the accurate analysis of the work of others must not be neglected. Finally, it must be remembered that it is practice, nothing but faithful practice, that makes an artist.

3. *Language.* We learn languages, not merely for the erudition and wisdom which they hold, but because languages are the instruments by which we acquire knowledge and by which we impart our knowledge to others. The study of languages, particularly in youth, should be joined to the study of objects. The intelligence should thus be exercised on matters which appeal to the interests and comprehension of children. They waste their time who place before children Cicero and the other great writers; for, if students do not understand the subject-matter, how can they master the various devices for expressing it forcibly? The time

[1] See in this connection Tarde's *Laws of imitation.* New York, 1900.

would be more usefully spent on less ambitious efforts, so correlated that the languages and the general intelligence might advance together step by step. Nature makes no leaps, neither does art, since art imitates nature.

Each language should be learned separately. First of all, the mother-tongue should be learned; then a modern language — that of a neighboring nation; after this, Latin; and, lastly, Greek and Hebrew. The mother-tongue, because of its intimate connection with the gradual unfolding of the objective world to the senses, will require from eight to ten years; a modern language may be mastered in one year; Latin in two years; Greek in one year; and Hebrew in six months.

There are four stages in the study of a language. The first is the age of babbling infancy, during which time language is indistinctly spoken; the second is the age of ripening boyhood, in which the language is correctly spoken; the third is the age of mature youth, in which the language is elegantly spoken; and the fourth is the age of vigorous manhood, in which the language is forcibly spoken.

4. *Morals.* If the schools are to become forging places of humanity, the art of moral instruction must be more definitely elaborated. To this end Comenius formulates the following pedagogic rules: —

All the virtues may be implanted in men.

Those virtues which are called cardinal virtues — prudence, temperance, fortitude, and justice — should first be implanted.

Prudence may be acquired through good instruction, and by learning the differences which exist between things and the relative value of those things. Comenius expresses agreement with Vives, that sound judgment must be acquired in early youth.

Children should be taught to observe temperance in eating, drinking, sleeping, exercising, and playing.

Fortitude is to be learned by the suppression of excessive desires — playing at the wrong time or beyond the proper time — and by avoiding manifestations of anger, discontent, and impatience. It is needful for the young to learn fortitude in the matter of frankness and endurance in toil. Children must be taught to work, and moral education must preach the gospel of work.

Lastly, examples of well-ordered lives in the persons of parents, teachers, nurses, and schoolmates must continually be set before the children, and they must be carefully guarded against bad associations.

5. *Religion.* In the scheme of education which Comenius outlines in the *Great didactic*, religion occupies the most exalted place; and while training in morals is accessory to religion, children must in addition be given specific instruction in piety. For this purpose definite methods of instruction are outlined. Instruction in piety must be of such a character as to lead children to follow God, by giving themselves completely up to His will, by acquiescing in His love, and by singing His praises. The child's heart may thus be joined to His in love through meditation, prayer, and examination. Children should early be habituated to the outward works which He commands, that they may be trained to express their faith by works. At first they will not understand the true nature of what they are doing, since their intelligence is not yet sufficiently developed; but it is

important that they learn to do what subsequent experience will teach them to be right.[1]

While Comenius was not willing to go as far as St. Augustine and the early church fathers in the matter of abolishing altogether the whole body of pagan literature from the school, nevertheless, he thought that the best interests of the religious education of the child required unusual precaution in the reading of pagan books. He reminds his readers that it is the business of Christian schools to form citizens, not merely for this world, but also for heaven, and that accordingly children should read mainly those authors who are well acquainted with heavenly as well as with earthly things.

Types of Educational Institutions

The modern fourfold division of education into kindergarten, elementary schools, secondary schools, colleges or universities was clearly foreshadowed by Comenius in the *Great didactic*. His philosophy of education comprehends a school of infancy, a school of the mother-tongue, a Latin school, and a university. These different institutions, he notes, are not merely to deal with different subjects, but they are to treat the same subjects in different ways, giving such instruction in all of them as will make true men, true Christians, and true scholars, although grading the instruction throughout to the age, capabilities, and previous training of the learners.

1. *School of infancy.* Comenius would have a

[1] For a more detailed account of Comenius' views on the religious education of children see the following chapter on the *School of infancy*.

mother's school in every home, where children may be given such training as will fit them at the age of six years to begin regular studies in the vernacular school. He prepared for the use of mothers during this period a detailed outline, which he published under the title, *Information for mothers, or School of infancy*. An analysis of this book is given in the following chapter on the earliest training of the child.

2. *School of the mother-tongue.* This covers the years from six to twelve, and includes all children of both sexes. The aim of this school is to teach the young such things as will be of practical utility in later life — to read with ease both printing and writing in the mother-tongue; to write first with accuracy, and finally with confidence in accordance with the rules of the mother-tongue; to compute numbers as far as may be necessary for practical purposes; to measure spaces, such as lengths, breadths and distances; to sing well-known melodies, and to learn by heart the greater number of psalms and hymns commonly used in the country. In addition, the children study the principles of morality, the general history of the world, the geography of the earth and principal kingdoms of Europe, elementary economics and politics, and the rudiments of the mechanical arts.

The six years of the school of the mother-tongue are graded into six classes, with a detailed course of study for each class. Provision is made for four lessons daily, two in the forenoon and two in the afternoon. The remaining hours of the day are to be spent in domestic work or in some form of recreation. The morning hours are devoted to such studies as train the intellect; the afternoons to such as give manual skill. No new work is to be introduced in the afternoon; but the pupils may review and discuss the lessons developed during the morning sessions. If it is desired that a foreign language be introduced, it should not be begun before the tenth year.

3. *The Latin school.* The purpose of the Latin school is to give a more thorough and comprehensive training to those aspiring to callings higher than the industrial pursuits. It covers the years from twelve to eighteen, and was also divided into six classes,— the grammar, natural philosophy, mathematical, ethics, dialectic, and rhetorical classes. Since Comenius' views on Latin are so fully set forth in a later chapter on language teaching and the *Janua*, it is only necessary here to recall that his curriculum for the Latin school includes a wide range of culture subjects. The most important of the culture studies of the Latin school is history, including an epitome of Biblical history, natural history, the history of arts, inventions and customs, history of morals, and a general historical survey of the leading modern nations of the world.

4. *University.* While Comenius frankly admits that his experience has been chiefly limited to work in elementary and secondary schools, still he sees no reason why he should not state his views and wishes with regard to superior instruction. The curriculum of the university conceived in the *Great didactic* is universal in character, making provision for a wide range of studies in every branch of human knowledge. The university must possess learned and able professors in the languages, sciences, and arts, as well as a library of well-selected books for the common use of all. One of the fundamental aims of the university

is to widen the domain of knowledge through original investigation; in consequence, its equipment must fit it for research work.

How fully these schemes have been realized, the reader may appreciate by comparing the types of educational institutions of the United States and Germany with those of the *Great didactic*, which were outlined by Comenius more than two centuries ago.

School Discipline

The *Great didactic* is an eloquent protest against the severe and inhuman discipline of Comenius' day. Schools which abound with shrieks and blows, he says, are not well disciplined. Discipline is quite another thing; it is an unfailing method by which we may make our pupils pupils in reality. This makes it necessary for the teacher to know the child, the being to be disciplined, the subjects of study which serve as mental stimulants, and the relations which should exist between the child and the subjects to be taught.

Discipline must be free from personal elements, such as anger or dislike, and should be exercised with frankness and sincerity. Teachers should administer punishments just as physicians prescribe medicines — with a view to improving the condition of the individual. Nor should severe forms of discipline be exercised in connection with studies or literary exercises. Studies, if they are properly taught, form in themselves a sufficient attraction. When this is not the case, the fault lies not with the pupil, but with the teacher; if his skill is unable to make an impression on the understanding, his blows will have no effect.

Indeed, he is more likely to produce a distaste for letters than a love for them by the application of force.

Whenever, therefore, we see a mind that is diseased or dislikes study, we should try to remove its disposition by gentle remedies; but on no account should we employ violent ones. The sun gives us an excellent lesson on this point. In the spring-time, when the plants are young and tender, it does not scorch them, but warms and invigorates them; it does not put forth its full heat until they are full grown. The gardener proceeds on the same principle, and does not apply the pruning knife to plants that are immature. In the same way the musician does not strike his instrument a blow with his fist or throw it against the wall because it produces a discordant sound; but setting to work on scientific principles, he tunes it and gets it into order. Just such a skilful and sympathetic treatment is necessary to instil a love of learning into the minds of pupils; and any other procedure will only convert their idleness into antipathy and their interest into downright stupidity.

Severe forms of discipline should be used only in cases of moral delinquencies, as (1) impiety of any kind, such as blasphemy, obscenity, and other offences against God's law; (2) stubbornness and premeditated misbehavior, such as disobeying orders and conscious neglect of duty; and (3) pride, disdain, envy, and idleness. Offences of the first kind are an insult against the majesty of God; those of the second kind undermine the foundations of virtue; and those of the third prevent any rapid progress in studies. An offence against God is a crime, and should be expiated by an extremely severe punishment; an offence against man desired result should not follow; (2) to teachers, who, without a knowledge of this art, try in turn first one plan and then another — a course which involves a tedious waste of time and energy; and (3) to schools, that they may become places of amusement, houses of delight and attraction, and that they may cause learning to flourish. Such, in brief, are fundamental principles of a philosophy of education. How well those principles were elaborated and applied will be seen in the exposition of his writings which follows.

Purpose of Education

The opening chapters of the *Great didactic* treat of man as the highest, the most absolute, and the most excellent of created beings: of the life beyond as man's ultimate end, and of this life as merely a preparation for eternity. The human being passes through three stages in his preparation for eternity — he learns to know himself, to rule himself, and to direct himself to God. Man's natural craving is for knowledge, — learning, virtue, piety, — and the seeds of knowledge are implanted in every rational creature. The mind of man is unlimited in its aspirations. "The body is enclosed by small boundaries; the voice roams within wider limits; the sight is bounded only by the vault of heaven; but for the mind, neither in heaven nor anywhere outside of heaven can a boundary be fixed for it."

Man delights in harmony; and, as respects both his mind and his body, he is a harmony. Just as the great world itself is like an immense piece of clockwork, put together with many wheels and bells, and arranged with such art that, throughout the whole

CHAPTER VII

EARLIEST EDUCATION OF THE CHILD

School of infancy — Circumstances under which written — View of childhood — Conception of infant education. Physical training — Care of the body — The child's natural nurse — Foods — Sleep — Play and exercise. Mental training — Studies which furnish the materials of thought, and studies which furnish the symbols of thought — Nature study — Geography — History — Household economy — Stories and fables — Principle of activity — Drawing — Arithmetic — Geometry — Music — Language — Poetry. Moral and religious training — Examples — Instruction — Discipline — Some virtues to be taught — Character of formal religious instruction.

The School of Infancy

PLATO, Quintilian, Plutarch, and other writers on education have discussed the earliest training of the child, but none of these early writers have comprehended the significance of infancy with any such pedagogic insight as Comenius; and his *School of infancy* has taken a permanent place among the classics which deal with the period of childhood. It was written during the years 1628 to 1630, when he was in charge of the Moravian school at Lissa. A German edition (it was originally written in the Sclavic tongue) appeared at Lissa in 1633, a second edition at Leipzig in 1634, and a third German edition at Nuremberg in 1636. Subsequently Polish, Bohemian, and Latin translations appeared; and Joseph Müller,[1] a most painstaking Comenius bibliographer, mentions an English translation in 1641.   I have found no other reference to an English translation so early.   As already noted, however, Comenius was well and favorably known to Milton, Hartlib, and others high in educational authority in England; and the fact that most of his other writings were translated there gives credence to Mr. Müller's statement.   In the year 1858, Mr. Daniel Benham[2] published in London an English translation, to which he prefixed a well-written account of the life of Comenius.   But his translation was soon out of print; and this excellent treatise in consequence remained inaccessible to English readers until the appearance of my own translation.   (Boston, 1896. Republished in London, 1897.)

The *School of infancy* was written as a guide for mothers during the first six years of the child's life, and was dedicated to " pious Christian parents, guardians, teachers, and all upon whom the charge of children is incumbent."   Since the education of the child must begin at its birth, mothers must assume the teacher's rôle; and the mothers of the seventeenth century, according to Comenius, were altogether unfitted because of lack of training to undertake this high and holy mission.   Accordingly, the *School of infancy* outlines definite instructions for mothers.

Comenius was too deeply grounded in the religious

---

[1] Zur Bückerkunde des Comenius. *Monatshefte der Comenius-Gesellschaft.* 1892. Vol. I., pp. 19-53.

[2] *School of infancy : an essay on the education of youth during the first six years, by John Amos Comenius.* To which is prefixed a sketch of the life of the author. London, 1858. pp. 168 + 75.

dogmas of his day to abandon altogether the doctrine of original sin, then so generally held; but he maintained that suitable early training would overcome most of the original perversity in the human heart. No one, he urges, should be a mother or a teacher who does not hold unbounded faith in the possibilities of childhood. The child is not to be regarded with reference to its youthful disabilities, but rather with a view to the purposes of the Divine mind, as Fröbel would say, regard the child as a pledge of the presence, goodness, and love of God. What higher tribute to childhood than this: "The mother that has under her care the training of a little child possesses a garden in which celestial plantlets are sown, watered, bloom, and flourish. How inexpressibly blessed is a mother in such a paradise!" With Quintilian he asks: "Has a son been born to you? From the first, conceive only the highest hopes for him."

The purpose in the education of the child is threefold: (1) faith and piety, (2) uprightness in respect to morals, and (3) knowledge of languages and arts; and this order must not be inverted. Parents, therefore, do not fully perform their duty when they merely teach their offspring to eat, drink, walk, and talk. These things are merely subservient to the body, which is not the man, but his tabernacle only; the rational soul dwells within, and rightly claims greater care than its outward tenement.

In the education of the child, care especially for the soul, which is the highest part of its nature; and next, attend to the body, that it may be made a fit and worthy habitation for the soul. Aim to train the child to a clear and true knowledge of God and all his wonderful works, and a knowledge of himself, so that he may wisely and prudently regulate his actions.

It must be borne in mind, however, that to properly train children requires clear insight and assiduous labor. It is to be regretted that so many parents are too incompetent to instruct their children and that others, by reason of the performance of family and social duties, are unable to discharge this high and holy mission. All such, of course, must hand their children over to some one else to instruct. But they should intrust their little ones to the care and training of such instructors only who will make the act of learning pleasing and agreeable — a mere amusement and mental delight.

Schools should be retreats of ease, places of literary amusement, and not houses of torture. A musician does not dash his instrument against the wall, or give it blows and cuffs because he cannot draw music from it, but continues to apply his skill until he is able to extract a melody. So by your skill you should bring the mind of the young child into harmony with his studies.

The first step in the education of the child is the most important. Every one knows that whatever form the branches of an old tree may have, that they must necessarily have been so formed from the first growth. The animal born blind, lame, defective, or deformed remains so. The training of the child's body, mind, and soul should, therefore, be a matter of earnest thought from the very first.

While it is possible for God to completely transform an inveterately bad man, yet, in the regular course of nature, it scarcely ever happens otherwise than that as a being is formed during the early stages of development, so it matures, and so it remains. Whatever seed is sown in youth, such fruit is reaped in old age.

Nor is it wise to delay such training until the child is old enough to be instructed in a school, since tendencies are acquired which are difficult to overcome. It is impossible to make a tree straight that has grown crooked, or to produce an orchard from a forest everywhere surrounded with briers and thorns. This makes it necessary for parents to know something about the management of children, that they may be able to lay the foundations upon which the teachers are to build when the child enters school at the age of six years.

Great care must be exercised with reference to the methods adopted with children so young. The instruction need not be apportioned to the same degree that it is apportioned in schools, since at this early age all children are not endowed with equal ability, some beginning to speak in the first year, some in the second, and some not until the third year.

Physical Training

The first care of the mother must be for the health of her child, since bodily vigor so largely conditions normal mental development. "A certain author," says Comenius, "advises that parents ought 'to pray for a sound mind in a sound body,' but they ought to labor as well as pray." Since the early care of the child devolves largely on the mother, Comenius counsels women with reference to the hygiene of childhood. Prenatal conditions are no less important than post-

I

natal; and prospective mothers should observe temperance in diet, avoid violent movements, control the
emotions, and indulge in no excessive sleep or indolence.

For good and sufficient reasons the mother should
nurse her own child. "How grievous, how hurtful,
how reprehensible," he exclaims, "is the conduct of
some mothers, especially among the upper classes, who,
feeling it irksome to nourish their own offspring, dele-
gate the duty to other women." This cruel alienation
of mothers from their children, he maintains, is the
greatest obstacle to the early training of the child.
Such conduct is clearly opposed to nature: the wolf
and bear, the lion and panther, nourish their offspring
with their own milk; and shall the mothers of the
human race be less affectionate than the wild beasts?
Moreover, it contributes to the health of the child to
be nourished by its natural mother.

Comenius has some sound advice for mothers on the
kinds of food for young children. At the first it must
as nearly as possible approximate to their natural ali-
ment; it must be soft, sweet, and easily digestible.
Milk is an excellent food; and after milk, bread,
butter, and vegetables. All highly seasoned foods are
to be avoided; and Comenius urges mothers to regard
medicines as they would poisons, and avoid them
altogether. Children accustomed to medicine from
their earliest years are certain to become "feeble,
sickly, infirm, pale-faced, imbecile, cancerous."

Children during the earliest years require an abundance of sleep, fresh air, and exercise. They need not
only to be exercised, but their exercises should be in
the nature of amusements. "A joyful mind," he
remarks, "is half health, and the joy of the heart is

the very life-spring of the child." These exercises for
the amusement of the child may provide for the pleasure of its eyes, ears, and other senses, as well as contribute to the vigor of its body and mind. Play not
only conduces to the health of the child, but it lays the
basis for later development.[1]

Mental Training

For the mental training of the child during its first
six years Comenius has outlined two classes of studies:
(1) those which furnish the materials of thought, such
as nature study, geography, and household economy,
and (2) those which furnish the symbols of thought,
such as drawing, writing, and language. This grouping of form and content studies, it should be noted,
has been followed by the disciples of Herbart in their
schemes of classification.

The first and second years of the child's life must
be entirely given over to the development of organic
functions; but, by the beginning of the third year, the
child has acquired a vocabulary, and he should be
taught to comprehend the meaning of the words he
uses. This early knowledge should be of natural
things — plants, flowers, trees, sand, clay, the cow,
horse, and dog. He may be taught to comprehend
some of the more important observable characters of
these objects and to know their uses.

Special exercises should be provided for the training

---

[1] To except Locke no reformer before Comenius' time has set
forth the need of physical training with anything like the clearness
and fulness of the *School of infancy*. See *Some thoughts concerning education by John Locke*. Edited with introduction and notes
by R. H. Quick. London, 1884. pp. 240.

of the eye; excessive lights must be avoided, and also overstraining.   Children may be moderately introduced to objects of color, and thus taught to enjoy the beauty of the heavens, trees, flowers, and running water.   In the fourth and following years they should be taken into fields and along the rivers, and trained to observe plants, animals, running water, and the turning of windmills.   In both nature study and geography Comenius anticipated the *Heimatskunde* of Pestalozzi.

Children should also during their first six years be taught to know the heavens, and to distinguish between sun, moon, and stars; to understand that the sun and moon rise and set; to recognize that the days are shortest in winter and longest in summer; to distinguish time — morning, noonday, evening, and when to eat, sleep, and pray.

The study of geography should be begun at the cradle, and the location, distance, and direction of the nursery, kitchen, bed-chamber, and orchard should early be learned.   They should have out-door lessons in geography, and be taught to find their way through the streets, to the market-place, and to the homes of their friends and relatives.   In the fifth year they should study a city, field, orchard, forest, hill, and river, and fix what they learn about these things in the memory.

The early historic instruction should begin with a development of the sense of time — the working days and the Sabbath days, when to attend and engage in divine services, the occurrence of such solemn festivals as Christmas, Easter, and Whitsuntide, and the significance of these holy occasions.   The child may also be trained to recall where he was and what he did yesterday, the day before, a week ago.

Household economy should receive important instruction during the first six years of the child's life. He must be trained to know the relation which he is to sustain to his father and mother, and to obey each; where to place and how to care for his clothes; the use of toys and playthings; the economy of the home, and his place in that economy.

Comenius also commends stories and fables, particularly those about animals which contain some moral principle. "Stories," says Comenius, "greatly sharpen the innate capacity of children." Ingeniously constructed stories serve a twofold purpose in the early development of the child: they occupy their minds, and they instil knowledge which will afterward be of use.

The greatest service which parents can render their children during these early years is to encourage play. This must not be left to chance, but must be provided for; and children need, most of all, to play with other children near their own age. In such social plays with their companions there is neither the assumption of authority nor the dread of fear, but the free intercourse which calls forth all their powers of invention, sharpens their wits, and cultivates their manners and habits.

In his discussion of the form studies, such as drawing, writing, and language, Comenius remarks that nothing delights children more than to be doing something. Youthful vigor will not long permit them to be at rest; and this spontaneous activity requires wise regulation, in order that children may acquire the habit

of doing things that they will be required to do later.[1]
This is the time when children are most imaginative
and imitative; they delight in doing the things that
they have seen done by their elders. All these imitative exercises give health to their bodies, agility to
their movements, and vigor to their muscles.

At this period children delight in construction; supply them with material with which they may exercise
whatever architectural genius they may have — clay,
wood, blocks, and stones, with which to construct
houses, walls, etc. They should also have toy car-
riages, houses, mills, plows, swords, and knives.
Children delight in activity, and parents should realize
that restraint is alike harmful to the development of
the mind and the body.

After children have been taught to walk, run, jump,
roll hoop, throw balls, and to construct with blocks and
clay, supply them with chalk or charcoal, and allow
them to draw according as their inclination may be
excited. In arithmetic Comenius recognizes the difficulty in leading children to see quantitative relations.
By the fourth year, however, he thinks that they may
be taught to count to ten and to note resemblances
and differences in quantity. To proceed further than
this would be unprofitable, nay, hurtful, he says, since
nothing is so difficult to fix in the mind of the young
child as numbers. Comenius, it would seem, valued
the study of arithmetic much less highly than modern
educators. He thought that some geometry might be
taught during these early years; children may easily

[1] Note the harmony of this conception of play with the modern
theories of Professor Karl Groos in his *Play of animals* (New York,
1898, pp. 341) and in his *Spiele der Menschen* (Jena, 1899, pp. 538).

be trained to perceive the common geometric forms; and the measurements and comparisons involved in the perception of such forms train the understanding of the child.

Music is instinctive and natural to the child. Complaints and wailings are his first lessons in music. It is impossible to restrain such complaints and wails; and even if it were possible, it would not be expedient, since all such vocalizations exercise the muscles involved in the production of speech, develop the chest, and contribute to the child's general health. Children should hear music in their earliest infancy, that their ears and minds may be soothed by concord and harmony. He even countenances the banging and rattling noises which children are fond of making, on the ground that such noises represent legitimate steps in the development of the child's musical sense. Give them horns, whistles, drums, and rattles, and allow them to acquire perceptions of rhythm and melody.

In the matter of instruction in language, Comenius had one fundamental principle — that ideas of things must accompany or precede the words which symbolized the things. In consequence, word training, as such, had no place in his schemes of education. When children begin to talk, great care must be exercised that they articulate distinctly and correctly. The start must always be in the mother-tongue. Comenius, it will be recalled, was at variance with his contemporaries in deferring instruction in Latin until the child was twelve years old. During these early years he believes that poetry — and especially jingles and nursery rhymes — may be used with great profit in aiding children to acquire language. They may not always understand the rhymes, but they are certain to be pleased much more by the rhythm of verse than by prose.

Moral and Religious Training

However much Comenius may have valued mental and physical training, the fundamental aim and end of all education he regarded as moral and religious. The agencies which he would have employed in the early moral training of the child are (1) a perpetual example of virtuous conduct; (2) properly timed and prudent instruction and exercise; and (3) well-regulated discipline. Children are exceptionally imitative, in consequence of which there should be great circumspection in the home in matters of temperance, cleanliness, neatness, truthfulness, complaisance, and respect for superiors. While lengthened discourses and admonitions are not expedient, prudent instruction may often accompany examples with profit.

As to discipline, Comenius thinks that occasionally there is need of chastisement in order that children may attend to examples of virtue and admonition. When other means of discipline have been ineffectual, the rod may be used, but only for offences against morals — never for stupidity. Comenius gives the impression that children may be whipped into being good. The influence of the ill-timed advice of Solomon is clearly apparent here.

Temperance and frugality, he thinks, claim the first place in the moral training of the child, inasmuch as they are the foundations of health and life, and the mother of all the virtues. Neatness and cleanliness should be exacted from the first; so should respect of superiors and elders. Bold and forward children are not generally loved. Obedience, like the plant, does not spring up spontaneously, but requires years of patient care and training to develop into a thing of beauty. Truthfulness likewise is no less important; so also justice, respect for the rights of others, benevolence, patience, and civility.

And most important of the virtues to be acquired by the young child is industry. Nothing hinders moral growth more than indolence. Comenius agrees with the church fathers that Satan's best allies are the idle. Children must not be idle. Teach them to play, to make things, to do things, to be helpful to themselves and useful to others.

Comenius exaggerated the importance of religious training during the child's earliest years. While recognizing that reasoning was necessary for the best results in religious instruction, he nevertheless overburdens the memory with formal religious instructions. Before the child is six years old he is to be taught the Lord's Prayer, the Apostles' Creed, the Confession of Faith, the Ten Commandments, and numerous hymns.

In spite of his unreasonable demands on the memory, most of Comenius' counsels to mothers on the religious instruction of their little ones are sane and helpful. The spirit of the parents, he rightly suggests, is all important in religious instruction; outward piety is not enough. The religious nature unfolds slowly, and unusual patience and foresight are required in its nurture and development.

All this training — physical, mental, moral, and religious — has been preliminary to the formal training in the school, which is to begin in the sixth or seventh year of the child's life. The transition step from the home to the school is now to be made ; for just "as little plants after they have grown up from their seed are transplanted into orchards, for their more successful growth, so it is expedient that children, cherished and nurtured in the home, having acquired strength of mind and body, should be delivered to the care of teachers."

CHAPTER VIII

STUDY OF LANGUAGE

Dominance of Latin in the seventeenth century — Methods of study characterized by Comenius. The *Janua* — Purpose and plan — Its success. *Atrium* and *Vestibulum* — Their relation to the *Janua*. The *Orbis pictus* — How conceived — Its popularity — Use of pictures. *Methodus novissima* — Principles of language teaching — Function of examples — Place of oral and written language in education.

RECALLING that Latin occupied such an exalted place in the schools of Comenius' day, it is not at all surprising that he gave so much attention to the study of language. Latin absorbed practically all the energies of the pupils, and with results that were far from satisfactory. A historian of the period says, " Boys and teachers were alike unhappy ; great severity of discipline was practised, and after all was done, and all the years of youth had been spent in the study mainly of the Latin, the results were contemptible."

The study of Latin is thus characterized by Comenius :

1. The Latin language is taught abstractly without a knowledge of the things which the words denote. Words should be learned in connection with things already known ; it is false to conclude that, because children know how to utter words, they therefore understand them.

2. The second evil in the study of language is driv-

ing children into the manifold intricacies of grammar
from the very first. It is a blunder to plunge them
into the formal statements of grammar on their first
beginning Latin. To make matters worse, the Latin
grammar is written in Latin. How should we adults
like it, if, in the study of Arabic, we had a grammar
written in the Arabic first put into our hands?

3. The third evil in the study of language is the
practice of compelling children to make impossible
leaps instead of carrying them forward step by step.
We introduce them from the grammar into Virgil and
Cicero. The sublimity of poetic style is beyond the
conception of boys, and the subject-matter of Cicero's
epistles not easy for grown men. It will be said that
the object is to place before children a perfect model
to which they may attain. It is right to aim at a
perfect model, when the aim is practicable, and if we
proceed gradually to the highest. But larger things
are with advantage postponed to lesser things; and
lesser things, if accommodated to the age of the
learners, yield greater fruits than large things. If
Cicero himself were to enter our schools and find boys
engaged with his works, Comenius believes that he
would be either amused or indignant.

Professor Laurie remarks that " when we bear in
mind the construction of the Latin grammars then in
use, — that of Alvarus, for example, having five hundred rules and as many exceptions, — we cannot be
surprised at the unanimous condemnation of the then
current methods of teaching, and the almost universal
lamentation over the wasted years of youth."

The Janua

We are now to see how Comenius proposed to reform these evils. " I planned a book," he says, " in which all things, the properties of things, and the actions and passions of things should be presented, and to each should be assigned its proper work, believing that in one and the same book the whole connected series of things might be surveyed historically, and the whole fabric of things and words reduced to one continuous context. On mentioning my purpose to some friends, one of them directed my attention to the Jesuit father's *Janua linguarum*, and gave me a copy. I leaped for joy; but on examination, I found that it did not fulfil my plan."

The *Janua* referred to by Comenius was that written by William Bateus, an Irish Jesuit, who was spiritual father at Salamanca, Spain. His *Janua* appeared in Spain prior to 1605. It contained twelve hundred short Latin sentences with accompanying Spanish translations. The sentences were made up of common Latin root-words, and no word was repeated. In 1615 an English-Latin edition appeared; and subsequently editions in French, German, and Italian. The object of Bateus in the publication of his *Janua* was to promote the spread of Christianity by enabling the heathen the more easily to learn to read the Latin.

It will thus appear that the plan of the *Janua lingu-arum reserata* of Comenius, the book that was destined to make his name known throughout the world, was not wholly original with the Moravian reformer. The name and to some extent the plan of the book had been suggested by the publication of the Jesuit.

The first edition of Comenius' *Janua* appeared in 1631.[1] In the numerous subsequent editions the author made important changes and additions. In subject-matter, the *Janua* comprehends the elements of all the sciences and arts. There are a hundred chapter headings with a thousand Latin sentences and their German equivalents arranged in parallel columns. The subjects treated cover a wide range — from the origin of the world to the mind and its faculties. The first chapter is an introduction, in which the reader is saluted, and informed that learning consists in this: to know distinctions and names of things. He is assured that he will find explained in this little book the whole world and the Latin language. If he should learn four pages of it by rote, he would find his eyes opened to all the liberal arts.

The second chapter treats of the creation of the world, the third of the elements, and the fourth of the firmament. In chapters five to thirteen inclusive, fire, meteors, water, earth, stones, metals, trees, fruits, herbs, and shrubs are treated. Animals occupy the next five chapters; and man — his body, external members, internal members, qualities and accidents of the body, ulcers and wounds, external and internal senses, the intellect, affections, and the will — the eleven following chapters. Nineteen chapters are

---

[1] I am indebted to Dr. William T. Harris for the use of the copy of the *Janua* belonging to the library of the Bureau of Education at Washington. It is a handsome Elzevir, bound in vellum, and published at Amsterdam in 1661. It contains 863 pages, 511 of which are given to the thousand parallel sentences in the five languages (Latin, French, Spanish, Italian, and German), in which the book appears. The remaining 352 pages are given to the lexicon-vocabularies in the different languages.

given to the mechanic arts. Twenty-one chapters deal with the house and its parts, marriage, the family, civic and state economy. Twelve chapters are assigned to grammar, dialectics, rhetoric, arithmetic, geometry, and the other branches of knowledge, describing briefly what they are; and ethics gets twelve chapters, a chapter being devoted to each of the twelve virtues. In the four succeeding chapters, games, death, burial, and the providence of God and the angels are treated. Chapter ninety-nine treats of the end of the world; and in the one-hundredth chapter Comenius gives some farewell advice, and takes leave of his reader.

Each chapter of the *Janua* is to be read ten times. In the first reading there is to be an accurate translation into the vernacular; at the second reading the whole is to be written out, Latin and vernacular, and the teacher is to begin conversation in the Latin tongue. At the third reading the teacher is to read the Latin aloud, and the pupils are to translate into the vernacular without seeing the printed page. At the fourth reading the grammar is to be written out and the words parsed. Special attention is to be given to the derivation of words at the fifth reading; the synonyms to be explained at the sixth; and the grammatical rules applied at the seventh. At the eighth reading the pupils are to learn the text by heart. The ninth reading is to be devoted to a logical analysis of the subject-matter; and the tenth and last reading is to be conducted by the pupils themselves. They are to challenge one another to repeat portions of the text.

In this ingenious manner Comenius applies his long-cherished pansophic theories to language teaching, the *Janua* being an application of ideas formulated in the

Great didactic. It is, however, more than an application of pansophic notions — it is an attempt to realize his oft-enunciated educational maxim that words and things should never be divorced, that knowledge of the language should go hand in hand with the knowledge of the things explained.

The success of the *Janua* was most unexpected, and no one was more surprised at its sudden popularity than Comenius himself. "That happened," he writes, "which I could not have imagined, namely, that this childish book was received with universal approbation by the learned world. This was shown me by the number of men who wished me hearty success with my new discovery; and by the number of translations into foreign languages. For, not only was the book translated into twelve European languages, since I myself have seen these translations (Latin, Greek, Bohemian, Polish, German, Swedish, Dutch, English, French, Spanish, Italian, and Hungarian), but also into the Asiatic languages — Arabic, Turkish, and Persian — and even into the Mongolian, which is understood by all the East Indies."

The *Janua*, more than any other book that he wrote, made Comenius' name familiar to scholars throughout the world, and for more than a century it was the most popular secondary-school text-book in use. How came this book to confer on its author such world-wide fame ? "Partly," answers Raumer, "from the pleasure found in the survey of the whole world, adapted both to young and old, and at a day when no great scientific requirements were made. Many were amused by the motley variety of the imaginations and investigations of the book ; by its old-fashioned grammatical, didactic,

and rhetorical discussions, and its spiritual extrava-
gances. The greatest influence was, however, exerted
by the fundamental maxim of the book — that the
knowledge of a language, and especially of the Latin,
should go hand in hand with a knowledge of the things
explained in it." [1]

Atrium and Vestibulum

The *Janua* was followed in 1633 by the *Atrium*. It
contains 427 short sentences somewhat more amplified
than in the *Janua*. In the introduction the teacher
promises to initiate the pupil into the mysteries of
wisdom, the knowledge of all things, the ability to do
right always, and to speak correctly of everything,
especially in Latin, which, as a common language to
all nations, is indispensable to a complete education.
The foundation of things is laid in the *Vestibulum*
(subsequently published); the *Janua* furnishes the
materials for the building; and the *Atrium* provides
the decorations. With the completion of these, pupils
may confer with the wisest authors through their
books, and through this reading they may become
learned, wise, and eloquent.

The second part treats of substantives, as the classification of things; the third part of adjectives, as the
modification of things; the fourth part explains pro-
nouns; in the fifth part verbs are introduced; the
sixth part discusses adverbs, the seventh part preposi-
tions, the eighth part conjunctions, and the ninth part
interjections. The tenth part contains examples of

[1] The *Janua* has lately been brought out in France in inexpen-
sive form by Professor A. C. Vernier of the College of Autun. (Autun, 1899. pp. 350.)

K

the derivation of words. The *Atrium* was intended as a simplified Latin grammar to be used with the graded system of language teaching outlined by Comenius.

The *Vestibulum*, although written and published after the *Janua* and *Atrium*, was intended as a first book or Latin primer. The *Janua* was found to be too difficult for the younger learners, and so this simple book was composed during his sojourn at Saros-Patak. The sentences were abbreviated, and they deal with simple things. The following are the chapter headings: (1) Concerning the accidents or qualities of things; (2) Concerning the actions and passions of things; (3) The circumstances of things; (4) Things in the school; (5) Things at home; (6) Things in the city; (7) Concerning the virtues. He expresses regret that he is unable to illustrate the text of the *Vestibulum* with cuts to amuse the pupils and enable them the better to remember, but says that he could find no artists competent to do the required illustrative work. He urges the teachers to supply the want of such cuts by explanations of the things, or by showing the things themselves. Without some such devices, the instruction must necessarily be lifeless. "The parallelism of the knowledge of words and things is the deepest secret of the method."

Orbis Pictus

The idea of the use of pictures in elementary school work was suggested to Comenius by Professor Lubinus, of Rostock, who edited in 1614 a Greek testament in three languages. He suggested reforms in the simplification of language instruction, and advised the construction of a book containing pictures of things, with a certain number of brief sentences attached to each, until all the words and phrases of Latin were exhausted.

While at Saros-Patak, he carried into effect the desires set forth in the *Vestibulum* with reference to an illustrated child's first Latin reader, although the book was not printed until some years later, because of unexpected difficulty in finding a skilful engraver in copper. In a letter to Michel Endter, of Nuremberg, who subsequently published the *Orbis pictus*, Comenius wrote in 1655 : "It may be observed that many of our children grow weary of their books, because they are overfilled with things which have to be explained by the help of words. The pupils, and often the teachers themselves, know next to nothing about the things."

The *Orbis pictus* was first published at Nuremberg in 1657 ; and, although the *Janua* had been received with well-nigh universal favor, its popularity was surpassed by the illustrated book. I have no means of knowing how many editions of the *Orbis pictus* have appeared during the last two hundred and fifty years. I have myself seen twelve different editions in the British Museum, Comenius-Stiftung, library of Harvard University, and elsewhere. These are : Nuremberg, 1657, Latin-German ; London, 1658, Latin-English ; Amsterdam, 1673, Latin-Dutch-German ; Nuremberg, 1679, Latin-German-Italian-French ; London, 1727, Latin-English ; Nuremberg, 1746, Latin-German ; London, 1777, Latin-German ; St. Petersburg, 1808, Latin-Russian-German ; New York, 1810, Latin-English ; Wroctawin, 1818, Latin-Polish-French-German ; Königsgratz, 1883, Latin-Bohemian-German-French ; Syracuse, 1887, Latin-English.

The purpose of the *Orbis pictus,* as indicated by Comenius in the preface, was:

1. To entice witty children to learn; for it is apparent that children, even from their infancy, are delighted with pictures and willingly please their eyes with them.   And it will be very well worth the pains to have once brought it to pass that scarecrows may be taken away out of wisdom's gardens.

2. This same little book will serve to stir up the attention, which is to be fastened upon things, and even to be sharpened more and more, which is also an important matter.   For the senses being the main guides of childhood (because therein the mind does not as yet rise to an abstract contemplation of things), they must evermore seek their own objects; if the objects are not present, the senses grow dull and flit hither and thither out of weariness.   But when the objects are present, they grow merry, wax lively, and willingly suffer themselves to be fastened upon them till the things be sufficiently discerned.   This book, then, will do a good piece of service in taking flickering wits and preparing them for deeper studies.

3. Children being thus interested and the attention attracted, they may be furnished with the knowledge of the most important things by sport and merry pastime.   In a word, this book will add pleasure to the use of the *Vestibulum* and *Janua,* for which end it was at the first chiefly intended.   The accounts of the things being given in the mother-tongue, the book promises three good things: (1) It will afford a device for learning to read more easily than hitherto, especially having a symbolical alphabet set before it, with pictures of the voices [creatures] to be imitated.   The young ABC

pupils will easily remember the force of every character by looking at the creatures, and the imagination will be strengthened. Having looked over a table of the chief syllables, the children may proceed to view the pictures and the inscriptions set under them. Simply looking upon the object pictured will suggest the name of the object and tell how the picture is to be read. Thus the whole book being gone over by the bare use of the pictures, reading cannot but be learned. (2) The book being used in the vernacular will serve for the perfect learning of the mother-tongue. (3) The learning of the vernacular words will serve as a pleasant introduction to the Latin tongue.

The *Orbis pictus* was translated for use in English schools in 1658 by Charles Hoole, a London schoolmaster. He observes in his introduction: "There are few of you (I think) but have seen, and with great willingness have made use of (or at least pursued), many of the books of this well-deserving author, Mr. John Comenius, which, for their profitableness to the speedy attainment of a language, have been translated into several countries, out of Latin into their native tongue. Now the general verdict (after trial made) that hath passed, touching those formerly extant, is this, that they are indeed of singular use, and very advantageous to those of more discretion (especially of such as already have a smattering of Latin) to help their memories to retain what they have scatteringly gotten here and there, to furnish them with many words, which (perhaps) they have not formerly read, or so well observed; but to young children (whom we have chiefly to instruct), as to those that are ignorant altogether of things and words, and prove rather a mere toil and burden, than a delight and furtherance. For to pack up many words in memory of things not conceived in the mind, is to fill the head with empty imaginations, and to make the learner more to admire the multitude and variety (and thereby to become discouraged) than to care to treasure them up in hopes to gain more knowledge of what they mean."

The first lesson in the *Orbis pictus* is a dialogue between a teacher and a pupil. The former says, " Come, boy, learn to be wise." Whereupon the latter asks, " What doth this mean ? " The master makes reply, " To understand rightly, to do rightly, and to speak rightly all that are necessary." The boy asks who will teach him these things, to which the master makes reply, " I, by God's help, will guide thee through all. I will show thee all; I will name thee all." To all this the boy makes eager response: " See, here I am. Lead me in the name of God." The master concludes the dialogue with this injunction: " Before all things thou oughtest to learn the plain sounds of which man's speech consisteth, which living creatures know how to make, and thy tongue knoweth how to imitate, and thy hand can picture out. Afterward we will go into the world, and we will view all things." Mr. Maxwell [1] thus characterizes this introduction and the picture that illustrates it: " The boy, a plump but not a pleasing person, and the master, a man ' severe ' and ' stern to view,' who has evidently all the frowns and none of the jokes of Goldsmith's schoolmaster. They are conversing on a barren plain, the only other living thing in sight being a wild ani-

[1] The text-books of Comenius. Proceedings of the National Educational Association for 1892. pp. 712–723.

mal apparently of some extinct species. In the background are a village church, of the regulation pattern, the roofs of houses, and a couple of pyramids which are intended for mountains."

The introduction is followed by an illustrated lesson on the sounds of the letters of the alphabet, with a picture and statement (in the vernacular and Latin) of the sounds made by animals. The crow illustrates the sound of *a*, the statement in the English being, "The crow crieth"; in the Latin, *Cornix cornicatur*. A lamb illustrates the sound of *b*, the statement being, "The lamb bleateth" (Latin, *Agnus balat*). And so on through the alphabet. This is what Comenius calls "a lively and vocal alphabet."

Like the *Janua*, the subjects treated in the *Orbis pictus* cover a wide range of topics. Their character may be indicated by the following citations of chapter headings: God, the world, the heavens, fire, the air, the water, the clouds, the earth, the fruits of the earth, metals, stones, trees, fruits of trees, flowers, potherbs, corn, shrubs, birds, tame fowls, singing birds, birds that haunt the fields and woods, ravenous birds, waterfowls, ravenous vermin, animals about the house, herd-cattle, laboring beasts, wild cattle, wild beasts, serpents and creeping things, crawling vermin, creatures that live as well by water as by land, river-fish and pond-fish, sea-fish and shell-fish, man, the seven ages of man, the outward parts of man, the head and the hand, the flesh and bowels, the charnels and bones, the outward and inward senses, the soul of man, deformed and monstrous people, dressing of gardens, husbandry, grazing, grinding, bread-making, fishing, fowling, hunting, butchery, cookery, the vintage, brewing, a feast, and so on to the one hundred and fifty-first chapter, in which the first illustration is reproduced with this benediction by the master: "Thus thou hast seen in short all things that can be shewed, and hast learned the chief words of the Latin and mother-tongue. Go on now and read other good books diligently, and thou shalt become learned, wise and godly. Remember these things: Fear God and call upon him that he may bestow upon thee the spirit of wisdom. Farewell."

Under the pictures illustrating each chapter follows the descriptions in the vernacular and the Latin. The following on the school may be taken as characteristic of the book: —

A school (1)
is a shop in which young wits are fashioned to virtue, and it is distinguished into classes.

The master (2)
sits in a chair (3)
the scholars (4)
in forms (5)
he teaches, they learn.

Some things are writ down before them with chalk on a table. (6)

Some sit
at a table and write (7)
he mendeth their faults (8)

Some stand and rehearse things committed to memory (9).

Some talk together (10) and behave themselves wantonly and carelessly; these are chastised with a ferrula (11)
and a rod (12)

Schola (1)
est officina in quâ novelli animi formantur ad virtutem & distinguitur in classes.

Præceptor (2)
sedet in cathedra (3)
discipuli (4)
in subselliüs (5)
ille docet, hi discunt.

Quædam præ scribuntur illis cretâ in tabella. (6)

Quidam sedent
ad mensam & scribunt (7),
ipse corrigit mendas (8).

Quidam stant & recitant mandata memoriæ (9).

Quidam confabulantur (10) ac gerunt se petulantes & negligentes; hi castigantur ferulâ (baculo) (11)
& virgâ (12).

The braced figures refer to the objects numbered in the cut; for example, a group of students conversing together in the illustration is marked 10 in the cut and in the text. The purpose of Comenius, it should be noted in passing, was primarily to teach the vernacular through things and the representation of things; although he had no objection to the learning of the Latin with the vernacular. His aim, as stated by himself, "That instruction may progress without hindrance, and neither learning nor teaching delay, since what is printed in words may be brought before the eyes by sight, and thus the mind may be instructed without error."

"Primer though it be," says G. Stanley Hall, "the *Orbis pictus* sheds a broad light over the whole field of education." Compayré remarks, "It was the first practical application of the intuitive method, and has served as a model for the innumerable illustrated books which for three centuries have invaded the schools." And Raumer, who is little given to praise of Comenius and his schemes, adds, " The *Orbis pictus* was the forerunner of future development, and had for its object, not merely the introduction of an indistinct painted world into the school, but, as much as possible, a knowledge of the original world itself, by actual intercourse with it."

Professor Laurie is doubtless right when he says that Comenius knew little psychology — scarcely more than the generalizations of Plato and Aristotle, and these not strictly investigated by himself. Yet who can read these lines in the preface of the *Orbis pictus*, " This little book will serve to stir up the attention, which is to be fastened upon things, and ever to be

sharpened more and more; for the senses ever more
seek their own objects, and when the objects are
present, they grow merry, wax lively, and willingly
suffer themselves to be fastened upon them, until the
things are sufficiently discerned " — who can read these
lines, and reflect upon the manner in which volitional
attention operates in the higher spheres of thought and
emotion, and say that Comenius was altogether ignorant of the psychological law that the power of the will
over the attention of little children is largely a matter
of automatic fixation, depending upon the attractive-
ness of the objects that affect the senses.

Methodus Novissima

While residing at Elbing, Comenius wrote the
Methodus novissima for the use of the teachers of
Sweden. This he intended as a plan of studies, and it
contains the principles which must lie at the basis of
every rational course of study. The three principles
of his method are the parallelism of things and words,
proper stages of succession, and easy natural progress.
In God are the ideas, the original types which he
impresses upon things; things, again, impress their
representation upon the senses, the senses impart
them to the mind, the mind to the tongue, and the
tongue to the ears of others; for souls shut up in
bodies cannot understand each other in a purely
intellectual way.

Any language is complete in so far as it possesses a
full nomenclature, has words for everything,— and
these significant and consistent,— and is constructed
in accordance with fixed grammatical laws. It is a

source of error when things accommodate themselves to words, instead of words to things. The same classification prevails for words as for things; and whoever understands the relation of words among themselves will, the more easily, study the analogous relations among things.

Vives thought that the most complete language would be that in which the words express the nature of things, and Comenius believed that there could be composed a real language in which each word should be a definition.

To be able to represent a thing by the mind, hand, or tongue is to understand it. The mental process involved consists of representations and images of the pictures of things. If, says Comenius, I perceive a thing by the senses, its image is impressed upon my brain; if I represent a thing, I impress its image upon the material; but if I express in words the thing which I have thought of or represented, I impress it upon the atmosphere, and through it upon the ear, brain, and mind of another.

Things are learned by examples, rules, and practice. Before the understanding, truth must be held up as an example; before the will, the good; before the forming powers, the ideal; and to these must be added practice regulated by suitable rules. But rules should not be given before the examples. This is well understood by artisans; they do not begin by lecturing to their apprentices upon trades, but by showing them how masters work and then by putting tools in their hands and training them to imitate their masters. We learn to do by doing, to write by writing, and to paint by painting.

The second step must never be taken until the first is learned; and the first step should be repeated and assimilated with the second step. We should advance from the easy to the more difficult, from the near to the more distant, and from the simple to the complex. Proceed toward knowledge by the perception and understanding of objects present to the senses, and later to the information of others about the objects.

The attention should be fixed upon one object at a time; first upon the whole, then upon the parts. The understanding should compare the objects being perceived with similar objects previously observed. The memory has three offices: to receive impressions, to retain impressions, and to recall impressions. Retention will be made easier by repetition, and recollection by the association of perceived relations. The youngest children should be instructed by means of visible objects, and pictures impress themselves most firmly upon the memory.

Teachers who are themselves intellectually quick must avoid impatience. The pupils who learn the quickest are not always the best; and the dulness of the pupils must be supplemented by the teacher's industry. Learning will be easy to pupils if teachers manage them in a friendly way and study the disposition of each child. Children must not only be made to look at their lessons, but to enter into the spirit of the subject under consideration.

We should remember that schools are the workshops of humanity; and that they should work their pupils into the right and skilful use of their reason, speech, and talents — into wisdom, eloquence, readiness, and shrewdness. Thus will the teachers shape these little

images of God, or, rather, fill up the outlines of goodness, power, and wisdom impressed upon them by
divine power. The art of teaching is no shallow
affair, but one of the deepest mysteries of nature and
salvation.

CHAPTER IX

INFLUENCE OF COMENIUS ON MODERN EDUCATORS

Francke — Early educational undertakings — The institution at
Halle — Character of the pædagogium — Impulse given to modern
learning.   Rousseau — The child the centre of educational
schemes — Sense training fundamental — Order and method of
nature to be followed.   Basedow — Protests against traditional
methods — Influenced by the *Émile* — His educational writings —
The Philanthropinum.   Pestalozzi — Love the key-note of his
system — Domestic education — Education for all classes and
sexes — The study of nature — Impulse given to the study of
geography.   Fröbel — His relations to Comenius and Pestalozzi —
Educational value of play and principle of self-activity — Women
as factors in education.   Herbart — Assimilation of sense-
experience — Training of character — Doctrine of interest.

It is less easy to trace the influence of Comenius on
modern educational reformers than to indicate the
traces of his pedagogic development, since he read
widely and credited cheerfully the paternity of his
educational ideals.   He says in this connection: "I
gave my mind to the perusal of divers authors, and
lighted upon many which at this age have made a
beginning in reforming the method of studies, as
Ratke, Helwig, Rheinus, Ritter, Glaum, Cæcil, and,
who indeed should have the first place, John Valentine
Andreæ, a man of noble and clear brain; as also Campanella and the Lord Verulam, those famous restorers
of philosophy; by reading of whom I was raised in
good hope, that at last those so many various sparks
would conspire into a flame; yet observing here and

there some defects and gaps, I could not contain myself from attempting something that might rest upon an immovable foundation, and which, if it could be once found out, should not be subject to any ruin. Therefore, after many workings and tossings of my thoughts, by reducing everything to the immovable laws of nature, I lighted upon my *Great didactic*, which shows the art of teaching all things to all men."

Such commendable frankness is not always found in the reformers that follow Comenius; but in their writings it is not difficult to discern community of ideas first definitely formulated by Comenius. This holds true in a degree of all reformers since Comenius' day, but in a measure sufficiently large to require passing note in Francke, Rousseau, Basedow Pestalozzi, Fröbel, and Herbart.

Francke [1]

Of a profoundly religious nature like Comenius, Francke applied himself to the study of theology at the Universities of Kiel and Leipzig, after having studied at Erfurt. The listless and heartless character of the teaching and study at these institutions impressed him profoundly, and directed his attention to the need of educational reform. Four years after taking his degree at Leipzig (1688), he established an infant school at Hamburg, which, though brief, was, as he tells us, the richest and happiest experience of his long and varied career. It taught him the lesson which he thought was needed alike by himself and his contemporaries —

[1] For a full account of Francke's life and work see *A. H. Francke's Pädagogische Schriften. Nebst einer Darstellung seines Lebens und seiner Stiftungen.* Herausgeg. von G. Kramer. Langensalza, 1876.

that teachers of little children entered upon their work with altogether too little preparation. He says, " Upon the establishment of this school, I learned how destructive is the usual school management, and how exceedingly difficult is the discipline of children; and this reflection made me desire that God would make me worthy to do something for the improvement of schools and instruction."

He received an ecclesiastical call to Erfurt, which he accepted, but his orthodoxy was questioned and he was not permitted to fill the office to which he had been appointed. The foundation of the University of Halle, in 1691, made an opening for him in the chair of Greek and Oriental languages. While serving in this capacity, he organized the philanthropic institution which has made Halle famous. It began as a charity work among the poor, and grew to such proportions that at his death, in 1727, — thirty-three years after its inception, — it included (1) the pædagogium with eighty-two students and seventy teachers and pupil-teachers; (2) the Latin school of the orphanage with three inspectors, thirty-two teachers, four hundred pupils, and ten servants; (3) elementary schools in Halle for the children of citizens, employing four inspectors, ninety-eight male and eight female teachers, and having an enrollment of one thousand and twenty-five children; (4) apothecary shops and bookstores. As a charity school, Francke's institution became the model of hundreds organized in Europe during the next century.

The pædagogium, which was a part of the great philanthropic institution, was opened in 1696, as a select school for the sons of noblemen. It was one

of the earliest training schools for teachers, and the
forerunner of university pedagogical seminaries,
which, in Germany at least, serve as training schools
for teachers in secondary schools. Francke aimed to
fit young men, and particularly university students,
in the faculties of philosophy and theology, for greater
usefulness as teachers. Indeed, much of the teaching
in the pædagogium was done by the university students who contemplated teaching careers. Besides the
practice work, instruction was given in the history
and theory of education, methods of teaching, and
school organization and government. Francke's pædagogium was a worthy progenitor of the long line of
renowned university seminaries which are now inte-
gral factors of the German universities, such, for
example, as the deservedly noted pedagogical seminary at Jena under the direction of Professor Wilhelm
Rein, and the not less noted pedagogical seminaries at
Leipzig under Professors Volkelt, Schiller, and Richter.

Like Comenius, Francke valued less the classical
culture, but more the modern learning which fitted for
the duties of life. "It is a common evil," he says,
"that we do not teach what we use in our occupations
every day." This led him to give large consideration
to the study of the mother-tongue. "I find few university students," he says, "who can write a German
letter correctly spelled. They violate orthography in
almost every line. I know of many examples where,
after they have entered upon the ministry and have
had occasion to have something printed, it has been
necessary to have their manuscripts first corrected in
almost every line. The reason for this defect is usually in the schools, where only the Latin translation

L

of their exercises is corrected, but not the German."
In many ways he labored to actualize the larger idea
of education which Comenius had outlined in the
Great didactic.

Rousseau

While he does not mention Comenius by name, even
a cursory reading of the *Émile*[1] furnishes abundant
evidence of Rousseau's familiarity with the writings
of the Moravian reformer, if not at first hand, then
through the writings of others. At any rate, some
striking parallels are suggested in a comparative study
of the writings of the two reformers. As summarized
by Mr. Davidson,[2] Rousseau's educational demands
are threefold: (1) the demand that children should,
from the moment of their birth, be allowed complete
freedom of movement; (2) that they should be educated through direct experience, and not through mere
information derived from books; (3) that they should
be taught to use their hands in the production of useful articles. These demands, it will be recalled, were
also made by Comenius in one form or another.

Comenius and Rousseau both emphasized the fact
that school systems must be made for children, and
not children for school systems. Neither reformer
shared the schoolmaster's customary contempt for

[1] An abbreviated translation of the *Émile* has been made by Miss
Eleanor Worthington (Boston: D. C. Heath & Co., 1891, pp. 157),
and a fuller (though not complete) translation by Professor William
H. Payne (New York: D. Appleton & Co., 1893. pp. 355).

[2] *Rousseau and education according to nature.* By Thomas
Davidson. New York: Charles Scribner's Sons, 1898. pp. 253.
Also the excellent life by John Morley, in two volumes (London and
New York, 1888).

childhood, but both urged that childhood must be studied and loved to be understood and trained, and both, if they had lived in the nineteenth and twentieth centuries, would have been enthusiastic advocates of child study. Says Rousseau: "We do not understand childhood, and pursuing false ideas of it, our every step takes us farther astray. The wisest among us fix upon what it concerns men to know, without ever considering what children are capable of learning. They always expect to find the man in the child, without thinking of what the child is before it is a man. . . . We never know how to put ourselves in the place of children; we do not enter into their ideas; we attribute to them our own; and following always our own train of thought, even with syllogisms, we manage to fill their heads with nothing but extravagance and error. . . . I wish some discreet person would give us a treatise on the art of observing children — an art which would be of immense value to us, but of which parents and teachers have not as yet learnt the very rudiments."

Sense training was fundamental in Comenius' scheme of primary education. Nature studies — plants, animals, and minerals — were introduced from the first, that the child might early cultivate his powers of observation, and form the habit of acquiring knowledge at first hand. Rousseau likewise lays great stress on sense training. "The faculties which become strong in us," he says, "are our senses. These, then, are the first that should be cultivated; they are, in fact, the only faculties we forget, or at least those which we neglect most completely. The child wants to touch and handle everything. By no means check

this restlessness; it points to a very necessary appren-
ticeship. Thus it is that the child gets to be conscious
of the hotness or coldness, the hardness or softness,
the heaviness or lightness of bodies, to judge of their
size and shape and all their sensible properties by
looking, feeling, listening, especially by comparing
sight and touch, and combining the sensations of the
eye with those of the fingers."

Comenius, Rousseau, and, in fact, all the realists
from Bacon to Herbert Spencer, have emphasized the
thought that education should follow the order and
method of nature; though, as Professor Payne suggests, it is not always easy to form a clear notion of
what they mean by nature, when they say that education should be natural, and that teachers should follow
the method of nature. The key-note of Rousseau's
theory, as expressed in the opening paragraph of the
Emile, is that "everything is good as it comes from
the hands of the author of nature, but everything
degenerates in the hands of man." Mr. Davidson
points out in his study of Rousseau that the air was
full of nature panaceas during the middle years of the
eighteenth century, and that these were applied alike
to social, political, and educational institutions. He
says: "The chief of these notions were (1) a state of
nature as man's original condition — a state conceived
sometimes as one of goodness, peace, freedom, equality,
and happiness, sometimes as one of badness, war,
slavery, inequality, and misery; (2) a law of nature
independent of all human enactment, and yet binding
upon all men; (3) a social contract, voluntarily and
consciously made, as the basis of justification for civil
society and authority — a contract by which men

united for the protection of rights and the enforce-
ment of laws which had existed already in the state
of nature; (4) false inequality among men, as due to
private property, or the usurpation by some of what,
by natural right, belonged to all; (5) a peaceful,
untroubled, unenterprising, unstruggling existence as
the normal form of human life."

While less sane, less practical, less comprehensive
in his educational views than Comenius, it can scarcely
be said that he was less influential. Differing in many
important particulars, a common ideal permeates the
writings of the two reformers — an unbounded faith
in the possibilities of youth, and a deep conviction that
it is the business of teachers to view the world and
nature from the standpoint of young and growing
children, and to cling with less tenacity to points of
view established by antiquity and convention.

Basedow

While resembling Rousseau more than Comenius in
temperament and character, as well as in educational
ideals, there is yet much in Basedow's educational
scheme that recalls the Moravian reformer. Born at
Hamburg, in 1727, he experienced, like Rousseau, an
unhappy childhood, and, like Comenius, received a
belated education. He prepared for the University of

[1] To except the brief sketch by Quick (*Educational reformers*,
pp. 273–289) and von Raumer's sketch in translation in Barnard's
American Journal of Education (Vol. 5, pp. 487–520), there is dearth
of material on Basedow in English. For an excellent account in
the German see *Pädagogische Schriften*. Mit Einleitungen, Anmerkungen, und Basedow's Biographie. Herausgegeben von Hugo
Göring. Langensalza, 1879–80.

Leipzig at the Hamburg gymnasium; but at both
institutions he rebelled against the traditional methods of instruction. After completing the course in
theology at Leipzig, it was found that he had grown
too heterodox for ordination, and he engaged himself
as a private tutor to a gentleman in Holstein.
Remarkable success attended his labors as a teacher.
He studied his children, adapted subject-matter to
their capacities, and made extensive use of conversa-
tional methods.   This experience secured him an
appointment in Denmark, where he taught for eight
years.   But his essays on *Methodical instruction in
natural and Biblical religion* disturbed alike the seren-
ity of the Danish clergy and schoolmasters, and
he was released and called to the gymnasium at
Altoona, where he encountered opposition no less
pronounced.

Rousseau's *Émile* appeared at this time, and it
influenced him powerfully. He renewed his attacks on
contemporary educational practices; charged universal
neglect of physical education and the mother-tongue;
criticised the schools for devoting so much time to the
study of Latin and Greek, and for the mechanical and
uninteresting methods employed in teaching these
languages; and admonished society for neglecting to
instruct the children of the poor and middle classes.
Raumer, who is no admirer of Basedow, admits the
justice of the charges.   He says: "Youth was in
those days for most children a sadly harassed period.
Instruction was hard and heartlessly severe.   Grammar was caned into the memory; so were portions of
Scripture and poetry. A common form of school punishment was to learn by heart the One Hundred and

Nineteenth Psalm. Schoolrooms were dismally dark. No one conceived it possible that the young could find pleasure in any kind of work, or that they had eyes for aught but reading and writing. The pernicious age of Louis XIV had inflicted on the children of the upper class hair curled by the barber and messed with powder and pomade, braided coats, knee breeches, silk stockings, and a dagger by the side — for active, lively children a perfect torture."

The publication, in 1774, of his *Elementary book with plates* and his *Book of methods* for parents and teachers, formulated and brought to public notice his views on education. The *Elementary book with plates* followed closely the lines of Comenius, and it has often been called the *Orbis pictus* of the eighteenth century. The purpose of the book was clearly ency-clopædic. As stated by himself, his aims were: (1) elementary instruction in the knowledge of words and things; (2) an incomparable method, founded upon experience, of teaching children to read without weariness or loss of time; (3) natural knowledge; (4) knowledge of morals, the mind, and reasoning; (5) a thorough and impressive method of instructing in natural religion, and for a description of beliefs so impartial that it shall not appear of what belief is the writer himself; (6) knowledge of social duties and commerce. The work was published in four volumes and illustrated by one hundred plates.

The *Book of methods* presents the root-ideas of Comenius and Rousseau. In it he says: "You should attend to nature in your children far more than to art. The elegant manners and usages of the world are, for the most part, unnatural. These come of themselves

in later years. Treat children like children, that they
may remain the longer uncorrupted. A boy whose
acutest faculties are his senses, and who has no perception of anything abstract, must first of all be made
acquainted with the world as it presents itself to the
senses. Let this be shown him in nature herself, or,
where this is impossible, in faithful drawings or
models. Thereby can he, even in play, learn how the
various objects are to be named. Comenius alone has
pointed out the right road in this matter. By all
means reduce the wretched exercises of the memory."

The institution which carried Basedow's educational
theories into practice was the Philanthropinum at
Dessau, which became both famous and notorious in
the days of the founder, and exercised, withal, a
powerful influence on the pedagogy of Germany and
Switzerland during the last quarter of the eighteenth
and the first half of the nineteenth century. Whatever may have been its faults, it had the merit of
looking at education from a more modern standpoint.
With the conviction that the final word had not been
spoken on pedagogy, Basedow boldly determined to
find new methods of approach to the child's mind.
As an experiment the Philanthropinum was both interesting and suggestive. Kant, who recognizes this
aspect of its utility, says: "It was imagined that
experiments in education were not necessary; but this
was a great mistake. Experience shows very often
that results are produced precisely the opposite to
those which had been expected. We also see from
experiments that one generation cannot work out a
complete plan of education. The only experimental
school which has made a beginning toward breaking

the path is the institution at Dessau. Whatever its faults, this praise must be given it: It is the only school in which teachers have had the liberty to work out their own methods and plans, and where they stood in connection, not only with each other, but with men of learning throughout all Germany."

In subjects taught, as well as in methods of teaching, Basedow followed Comenius in the main. Words were taught in connection with things; object teaching occupied an important place; pictures were extensively used; children were first taught to speak and later to write in foreign languages; German and French held positions of honor; arithmetic, geometry, geography, and natural history were all taught; great attention was given to the physical development of the children, and play was considered as important as Latin; school hours were shortened; the discipline was much less severe; and the children were allowed and permitted to take degrees of freedom altogether unheard of before Basedow's day.

Pestalozzi [1]

Pestalozzi was not widely read in the literature of education; in fact, the *Émile* was about the only such book he ever read, as he himself tells us. It is,

[1] There is a wealth of material in the English language on Pestalozzi. See: *Pestalozzi and the modern elementary school*, by Professor A. Pinloche (New York: Charles Scribner's Sons, 1900); *Pestalozzi: his life and work*, by Roger de Guimps (New York: D. Appleton & Co., 1897, pp. 438); *Life, work, and influence of Pestalozzi*, by Hermann Krusi (New York: American Book Co., pp. 240); and the rich volume of sources by Henry Barnard, *Pestalozzi and Pestalozzianism* (Hartford, 1859, pp. 238 + 230).

nevertheless, apparent that he was quite as much influenced by Comenius as by Rousseau. The vital principle of his reforms — love of and sympathy for the child — had been as forcefully enunciated by Comenius as by Rousseau; and the saner and more practical character of Pestalozzi's enthusiasm would lead one to suppose that he was less influenced by the author of the *Émile* than by the Moravian reformer. "The first qualification for the task [of teaching]," says Pestalozzi, in a letter to Greaves,[1] "is *thinking love*." And this spirit dominated all his efforts in behalf of educational reform. He says: "It is recorded that God opened the heavens to the patriarch of old, and showed him a ladder leading thither. This ladder is let down to every descendant of Adam; it is offered to your child. But he must be taught to climb it — not by the cold calculations of the head, or by the mere impulses of the heart, but by a combination of both."

Both reformers started with the child at birth, and made domestic education fundamental to their schemes. "Maternal love," says Pestalozzi, "is the first agent in education. Nature has qualified the mother to be the chief factor in the education of the child." In *How Gertrude teaches her children*[2] he tells us, "It is the main design of my method to make home instruction again possible to our neglected people, and to induce every mother whose heart beats

[1] *Letters on early education.* Addressed to J. P. Greaves, Esq., Syracuse, 1898, pp. 180.

[2] Translated by Lucy E. Holland and Frances E. Turner, and edited with introduction and notes by Ebenezer Cook. Syracuse: C. W. Bardeen, 1894. pp. xliv + 256.

for her child to make use of my elementary exercises."
Again, in the account of his school at Stanz, he says:
"My aim was to simplify teaching so that the common
people might be induced to begin the instruction of
their children, and thus render superfluous the teaching of the elements in the schools. As the mother is
the first to nourish her child physically, so also, by
the appointment of God, she must be the first to give
it spiritual and mental nourishment. I consider that
very great evils have been occasioned by sending children too early to school; and by adopting so many
artificial means of educating them away from home.
The time will come, so soon as we shall have simplified instruction, when every mother will be able to
teach, without the help of others, and thereby, at the
same time, go on herself always learning." This, it
will be recalled, was also Comenius' cherished desire
in the *School of infancy*.

Comenius and Pestalozzi stand almost alone among
the great educational reformers in proclaiming the
doctrine of universal education — training for the poor
as well as the rich, for the lowly born as well as for
the privileged classes, for girls as well as boys.
"Popular education," says Pestalozzi, "once lay before
me like an immense marsh, in the mire of which I
waded about, until I had discovered the source from
which its waters sprang, as well as the causes by
which their free course is obstructed, and made myself
acquainted with those points from which a hope of
draining its pools might be conceived. Ever since my
youthful days, the course of my feelings, which rolled
on like a mighty stream, was directed to this one point,
— to stop the sources of that misery in which I saw

the people around me immersed." Such regeneration
he thought could be brought about by consecrated and
intelligent schoolmasters, and particularly, as G. Stanley Hall notes in his admirable introduction to the
American translation of *Leonard and Gertrude*,[1] "by
the love and devotion of noble women overflowing
from the domestic circle into the community, by the
good Gertrudes of all stations in life, the born educators of the race, whose work and whose 'key-words'
we men pedagogues must ponder well if our teaching
is to be ethically inspired."

The study of nature, and this at first hand, was likewise an inheritance from Comenius. Pestalozzi makes
observation the basis of all knowledge. "If I look
back and ask myself what I have really done toward
the improvement of methods of elementary instruction,
I find that in recognizing observation as the absolute
basis of all knowledge, I have established the first and
most important principle of instruction. I have endeavored to discover what ought to be the character
of the instruction itself, and what are the fundamental
laws according to which the education of the human
race must be determined by nature."

Comenius was the first of the educational reformers
to recognize the importance of geography as a subject
of school study; and although he had it taught in the
schools he conducted, and gave it important consideration in his educational schemes, the study received
no fresh recognition until the time of Pestalozzi.
At Stanz, at Burgdorf, and at Yverdon, geography
ranked as one of the foremost elementary school

---

[1] Translated and abridged by Eva Channing. With an introduction by G. Stanley Hall. Boston: D. C. Heath & Co., 1897. pp. 181

studies. And not only was geography taught in the schoolrooms, but better than that, it was taught in the open air. Vulliemin, ¡who was two years a student under Pestalozzi at Yverdon, writes: "The first elements of geography were taught us on the ground. We began the study by taking a walk along a narrow valley on the outskirts of Yverdon. We were led to observe all its details, and then to help ourselves to some clay we found there. This we carried back in our baskets, and, on our return home, we had to make a model of the ground walked over, and of the surrounding country; this we did on long tables. Our walks were extended, from time to time, and, on our return, we added new features as we learned them."

Pestalozzi was fortunate in having with him at Yverdon two eminently successful German teachers, who comprehended his aims, and who subsequently applied his methods in the fatherland. One was Hennig, the author of a popular pedagogic work on home geography, and the other was Karl Ritter, the deservedly renowned German geographer. Ritter brought with him to Yverdon two young men from Frankfort whom he was tutoring, and he served Pestalozzi in the capacity of a pupil-teacher; and, while a developed man when he entered the institution, in 1807, he came to Yverdon, as so many other enthusiastic Germans had done, to study pedagogy with the most distinguished master of the century. Years later, when Ritter had become the best-known geographer of his age, he wrote: "Pestalozzi knew less geography than a child in one of our primary schools, yet it was from him that I gained my chief knowledge of this science; for it was in listening to him that I first conceived the idea of the natural method. It was he who opened the way to me, and I take pleasure in attributing whatever value my work may have entirely to him."

Comenius and Pestalozzi had much in common in their aims as educational reformers; and they together share, as Dr. Hoffmeister[1] points out, the honor of having originated and carefully elaborated one of the most efficient elementary school systems in Europe — the Volksschule in Germany. Pestalozzi gave himself to education, or, to use his own significant characterization, "I have lived all my days like a beggar, that I might teach beggars how to live like men." Comenius gave himself, also, and he gave besides a half-dozen books, which take classic rank in the permanent literature of education.

Fröbel

The large obligations of the founder of the kindergarten to both Comenius and Pestalozzi cannot be gainsaid. Fröbel's attention was called to the writings of the Moravian reformer early in his educational career by Professor Krause, Herder, and others interested in his schemes. "Comenius proposes an entirely new basis of education," Professor Krause wrote to Fröbel. "He attempts to find a method of education, consciously based upon science, whereby teachers will teach less, and learners will learn more; whereby there will be less noise in the schools, less distaste, fewer idle pupils, more happiness and progress; whereby confusion, division, and darkness will give place to order, intelligence, and peace." He adds, "Comenius

---

[1] *Comenius und Pestalozzi als Begründer der Volksschule.* Von Hermann Hoffmeister. Berlin, 1877.

was the first to advocate Pestalozzi's doctrine of observation (Anschauung)." Mr. Hauschmann,[1] one of Fröbel's biographers, remarks: "Krause looked upon Fröbel as the educational successor of Comenius and Pestalozzi. Fröbel, he thought, might show, as it had never been shown before, how the Pestalozzian doctrine of Anschauung was to be applied to the education of every child."

The weeks spent with Pestalozzi in the autumn of 1805 and the two subsequent years (1808–1810) passed with him at Yverdon, gave Fröbel ample opportunity to study thoroughly the Swiss reformer's theories and practices; and these he subsequently applied with even greater skill than his master had done. Schmid, the German historian of education, says, "Fröbel, the pupil of Pestalozzi, and a genius like his master, completed the reformer's system; taking the results at which Pestalozzi had arrived through the necessities of his position, Fröbel developed the ideas involved in them, not by further experience, but by deduction from the nature of man, and thus he attained to the conception of true human development and to the requirements of true education."

He was thus, in a sense, the combined product of the philosophy of Comenius and the zeal of Pestalozzi, although working along lines carefully marked out by himself. It does not detract from the fame of Fröbel to say that most of the root-ideas of his kindergarten are to be found in the *School of infancy*. Mr. Bowen,

[1] *The kindergarten system: its origin and development as seen in the life of Friedrich Fröbel*. By Alexander Bruno Hauschmann. Translated and adapted by Fanny Franks. London: Swan Sonnenschein & Co., 1897. pp. xvi + 253.

who has given us one of the best expositions [1] of
Fröbel's ideas, pays a just tribute of the obligation of
his master to the writings of Pestalozzi and Comenius.
He says: "With all his enthusiasm for education and
his desire to found it on a scientific basis, Comenius
had but little scientific knowledge of child-nature, and
troubled himself not at all to acquire it.   He constantly insisted, it is true, upon the exercise of the
senses, and an education in accordance with nature;
but his exercise of the senses soon reduced itself, in the
main, to the use of pictures, with a view to a readier
and more intelligent acquirement of language; and,
even in his *ergastula literaria,* or literary workshop,
the manual and other work introduced was intended
to aid poor children in partly getting their own living
while at school, rather than to exercise faculty; while
his 'nature' was as quaint and conventional as that
in a pre-Raphaelite picture.   *None the less, however,
Comenius was the true founder of educational method.*"

There is entire agreement in a few of the most fundamental aims of the two reformers.   Comenius, no
less than Fröbel, preached the gospel of self-activity,
and demanded that play be given important consideration in the training of the child.   What Comenius
says on these subjects has already been given in the
exposition of the *School of infancy.*   In his *Education
of man,* [2] Fröbel says: "Play is the purest, most spiritual activity of the child at this period; and, at the
same time, typical of human life as a whole — of the

---

[1] *Fröbel and education through self-activity.*   By H. Courthope
Brown.   New York: Charles Scribner's Sons, 1897.   pp. 209.

[2] Translated and annotated by W. N. Hailmann.   New York:
D. Appleton & Co., 1887.   pp. 332.

hidden natural life in man and all things. It gives, therefore, joy, freedom, contentment, inner and outer rest, peace with the world. A child that plays thoroughly, with self-active determination, perseveringly, until physical fatigue forbids, will surely be a thorough, determined man, capable of self-sacrifice for the promotion of the welfare of himself and others. Is not the most beautiful expression of child-life at this time a playing child? — a child wholly absorbed in his play? — a child that has fallen asleep while so absorbed? . . . The plays of the child contain the germ of the whole life that is to follow; for the man develops and manifests himself in play, and reveals the noblest aptitudes and the deepest elements of his being."

Fröbel joined with Comenius in demanding that women shall take a responsible part in the education of the child. Mr. James L. Hughes [1] says in this connection: "The greatest step made toward the full recognition of woman's individuality and responsibility since the time of Christ was made when Fröbel founded his kindergartens and made women educators outside the home — educators by profession. This momentous reform gave the first great impetus to the movement in favor of women's freedom, and provided for the general advance of humanity to a higher plane by giving childhood more considerate, more sympathetic, and more stimulating teachers." Fröbel was convinced that women were better adapted than men for the early stages of instruction. He says: "All agree that, compared with the true mother, the formal

[1] *Fröbel's educational laws for all teachers.* By James L. Hughes. New York: D. Appleton & Co., 1897. pp. 296.

M

educator is but a bungler. But she must become conscious of her own aim, and must learn intelligently the means to reach it. She can no longer afford to squander or neglect the earliest years of her child. As the world grows older, we become richer in knowledge and art. But childhood remains short as before."

In other important particulars Fröbel owed much to Comenius, as well as to Pestalozzi. Compare, for example, the *School of infancy* with the aims of the kindergarten, and the bequests of the Moravian reformer will at once be apparent. The exaggerated and unpedagogic symbolism, however, with which Fröbel burdened his otherwise excellent kindergarten system, formed no part of his heritage from Comenius.

Herbart

Professor De Garmo,[1] who has given us a most succinct statement of Herbart's educational views, remarks, "that one of the main results of Comenius, Rousseau, and Pestalozzi is the firmly fixed conviction that observation, or the use of the senses, and, in general, the consideration of simple concrete facts in every field of knowledge, is the sure foundation upon which all right elementary education rests. This truth is now the acknowledged starting-point of all scientific methods of teaching. Yet the fact of importance of observation in instruction does not carry with it any information showing how the knowledge so obtained can be utilized, or what its nature, time, amount, and order of presentation should be. In

[1] *Herbart and the Herbartians.* By Charles De Garmo. New York: Charles Scribner's Sons, 1895. pp. 268.

short, it does not show how mental assimilation can best take place, or how the resulting acquisitions can be made most efficiently to influence the emotional and volitional sides of our nature. Perception is, indeed, the first stage of cognition, but its equally important correlative is apperception and assimilation. It is Herbart and his successors who have made us distinctly conscious of this fact." There can be no reasonable doubt but that Herbart did give a powerful impulse to the judicious assimilation of acquired sense-experience; and yet even here it is quite possible to underestimate the character and value of the nature studies of Comenius and the object lessons of Pestalozzi.

Herbart, like Comenius, emphasized the necessary effect of all instruction on character. "The circle of thought," says Herbart, "contains the store of that which by degrees can mount by the steps of interest to desire, and then, by means of action, to volition. Further, it contains the store upon which all the workings of prudence are founded — in it are the knowledge and care, without which man cannot pursue his aims through means. The whole inner activity, indeed, has its abode in the circle of thought. Here is found the initiative life, the primal energy; here all must circulate easily and freely, everything must be in its place, ready to be found and used at any moment; nothing must lie in the way, and nothing like a heavy load impede useful activity." Indeed, as Kern suggests, in Herbart's scheme interest is the moral monitor and protector against the servitude that springs from passions and desires.

The doctrine of interest, but vaguely suggested by

Comenius, is perhaps the most noteworthy contribution of Herbart to modern pedagogy; but to summarize Herbart's views on interest would be to summarize his whole theory of education. He recognizes two groups of interests — intellectual and social. Two phases of intellectual interests are distinguished: (1) empirical interests, or the pleasures occasioned by disinterested curiosity; (2) speculative interests occasioned by the impulse to search out causal relations; and (3) æsthetic interests aroused through beauties in nature, art, and character. The social interests are likewise threefold: (1) sympathetic or altruistic; (2) social and fraternal; and (3) religious.

Herbart's contribution to empirical psychology, although important, was second to his application of direct pedagogic problems to actual school practice — the working out of his doctrine of many-sided interest, the selection and adjustment of materials of instruction, and the reform of school government and discipline.[1]

[1] See Herbart's *Science of education*. Translated from the German, with a biographical introduction by Henry M. and Emmie Felkin. Boston: D. C. Heath & Co., 1895. pp. 268.

CHAPTER X

PERMANENT INFLUENCE OF COMENIUS

General neglect of Comenius during the eighteenth century—
Causes—Intrenchment of humanism—Summary of the permanent reforms of Comenius—Revived interest in his teachings—
National Comenius pedagogical library at Leipzig—The Comenius Society—Reviews published for the dissemination of the
educational doctrines of Comenius—Conquest of his ideas.

THE permanent influence of Comenius remains to
be noted. Famous in his own day; enjoying the
friendship of great scholars and the confidence of royal
personages; the founder of numerous school systems;
the author of more than a hundred books and treatises,
which were translated into most of the languages of
Europe and Asia, — the name of the great Moravian
reformer was quite if not entirely forgotten, and his
writings practically unknown, for more than a century
after his death. Professor Nicholas Murray Butler,[1]
in likening him unto the stream that loses itself in the
arid desert and then reappears with gathered force
and volume to lend its fertilizing power to the surrounding country, says: "Human history is rich in
analogies to this natural phenomenon; but in Comenius
the history of education furnishes its example. The
great educational revival of our century, and particularly of our generation, has shed the bright light of

[1] *The place of Comenius in the history of education.* **Proceedings of the National Education Association for 1892. pp. 723-728.**

scholarly investigation into all the dark places, and
to-day, at the three hundredth anniversary of his
birth, the fine old Moravian bishop is being honored
wherever teachers gather together and wherever education is the theme."

The world, which usually takes pause for a moment,
when a great man dies, to seriously consider what
there was in the dead that lifted him above the ordi-
nary level, took no such inventory when the remains
of Comenius were laid at rest in a quiet little town in
Holland. "The man whom we unhesitatingly affirm,"
says Mr. Keatinge, "to be the broadest-minded, the
most far-seeing, the most comprehensive, and withal
the most practical of all writers who have put pen to
paper on the subject of education; the man whose
theories have been put into practice in every school
that is conducted on rational principles; who embodies
the materialistic tendencies of our 'modern side'
instructors, while avoiding the narrowness of their
reforming zeal; who lays stress on the spiritual aspect
of true education, while he realizes the necessity of
equipping his pupils for the rude struggle with nature
and with fellow-men — Comenius, we say, the prince
of schoolmasters, produced, practically, no effect on
the school organization and educational development
of the following century."

The causes of this universal neglect are not easily
explained. That he lived most of his days in
exile; that he belonged to a religious community
which was numerically insignificant and which suf-
fered all those bitter persecutions following in the
train of the Thirty Years' War; that indiscretion
entangled him in certain alleged prophetic revelations,

which subsequently turned out the baldest impostures; and, more important than all, as Professor Laurie points out, that schoolmasters did not wish to be disturbed by a man with new ideas, — these facts help to explain the universal neglect into which his name and writings fell.   In a personal letter, Oscar Browning expresses the belief that if the teachings of Comenius had been dated a century earlier, that the realistic type of education might have been generally followed — at least in the countries that had broken with the Church of Rome.   As it was, however, Melanchthon, the schoolmaster of the Reformation, adopted, with slight modifications, the humanistic type of education.   For the time being, at least, the ideas held by Comenius were pushed into the background, and humanism, already deeply intrenched, dominated educational practices.   Reformers were not wanting, however, to champion the reforms of Comenius, men like Francke, Rousseau, Basedow, Pestalozzi, Fröbel, and Herbart.   But it remained for the nineteenth century to realize, in considerable measure, the aims and aspirations of the far-reaching reforms of the Moravian bishop.

"There is nothing startling about the educational reforms of Comenius to-day," says Professor Earl Barnes.   "They are the commonplace talk of all school conventions.   But to see them when no one else has formulated them, to enunciate them before an audience often hostile, and to devote a life to teaching them and working them out — this requires a broad mind and something of the spirit of the martyr, and both these elements were strong in Comenius."

In spite of the neglect into which the reforms of

Comenius fell, his influence has been lasting because his work was constructive and his reforms were far reaching. Among the reforms which he advocated (and since incorporated in the modern educational movement), the following may be named: —

1. That the purpose of education is to fit for complete living, in consequence of which its benefits must be extended to all classes of society.

2. That education should follow the course and order of nature, and be adapted to the stages of mental development of the child.

3. That intellectual progress is conditioned at every step by bodily vigor, and that to attain the best results, physical exercises must accompany and condition mental training.

4. That children must first be trained in the mother-tongue, and that all the elementary knowledge should be acquired through that medium.

5. That nature study must be made the basis of all primary instruction, so that the child may exercise his senses and be trained to acquire knowledge at first hand.

6. That the child must be wisely trained during its earliest years, for which purpose mothers must be trained for the high and holy mission of instructing little children, and women generally be given more extended educational opportunities.

7. That the school course must be enriched by the addition of such useful studies as geography and history.

8. That the subjects of study must be so correlated and coördinated that they may form a common unit of thought.

9. That teachers must be specially trained.

10. That schools must be more rationally graded and better supervised.

11. That languages must be taught as "living organic wholes fitted for the purposes of life, and not as the lifeless tabulations of the grammarians."

It was the opinion of Mr. Quick that the most hopeful sign of the improvement of education was the rapid advance in the last thirty years of the fame of Comenius, and the growth of a large literature about the man and his ideas. The revival of Comenian ideas really dates from the beginning of the present century, when Germany, crushed and dismembered, looked to her schools as the surest means of regaining fallen glory; so that the battle of Jena may be given as the date of this awakened interest in the reforms of the Moravian educator. This interest culminated in the foundation of the great national Comenius peda-gogical library (Comenius-Stiftung) at Leipzig, in 1871. It was founded by a band of enthusiastic disciples of Comenius, of whom Julius Beeger was the foremost; and, although it numbered but 2642 volumes at the end of the first year, the interest in the movement has been so great that it now numbers over 70,000 volumes, and constitutes the largest single collection of pedagogical books in the world. The books are classified in 56 departments, the most important of which are: encyclopædias of pedagogy, complete collections of the writings of standard educational writers, sources of history of education, general works on the history of education, histories of special periods in education, histories of education in different countries, histories of individual educational institutions, educational biographies, works on systematic pedagogy, physical education, etc. The library covers every department of educational thought, and is especially strong in the literature relating to the elementary schools of Germany. The privileges of the library are freely open to all students of education. The library is under the control of the Leipzig teachers' association, and is sustained in part by the association and in part by appropriations from the city of Leipzig and the kingdom of Saxony.[1] What more appropriate memorial to the long and devoted life of Comenius to the cause of education could be desired, and what stronger evidence of the permanent influence of his work and worth.

A second recent manifestation of the permanency of the Moravian educator's influence is the Comenius Society (Comenius-Gesellschaft), with headquarters in Germany, and numbering among its members most of the leaders in educational thought in the world. It was organized in 1891. The objects of the society are (1) to spread the living influence of the spirit of Comenius and the men who have represented cognate reforms; (2) to work toward an increased knowledge of the past and a healthy development of the future on the principle of mutual union and forbearance, by means of the cultivation of the literature which has grown out of that spirit; and (3) to prepare the way for a reform of education and instruction on the lines laid down by Comenius. In order to realize these

[1] An excellent account of the national Comenius pedagogical library will be found in: *Die pädagogischen Bibliotheken, Schulmuseen und ständigen Lehrmittelausstellungen der Welt*. Von Julius Beeger. Leipzig: Zangenberg & Himly, 1892. pp. 84.

objects, the society further proposes (1) the publication of the more important writings and letters of Comenius and his associates; (2) inquiry into the history and dogmas of the old evangelical congregations (Waldenses, Bohemian Brethren, Swiss Brethren, etc.), chiefly by publishing the original sources from their history; and (3) the collection of books, manuscripts, and documents which are important for the history of the above objects.

The membership of the society, while overwhelmingly German, includes a considerable number from Austria-Hungary, Holland, Great Britain, the United States, Russia, Sweden, Norway, Italy, Switzerland, France, Greece, Belgium, and Denmark. The society inspired the numerous celebrations in commemoration of the three hundredth anniversary of the birth of Comenius (March 28, 1892). These celebrations, held at most of the educational centres in the Old World, and at a number of places in the New, revived the memory of Comenius, and brought his teachings to thousands of teachers who had known him before only as a name.

The society began in 1892 the publication of a high-grade review, — *Monatshefte der Comenius-Gesellschaft*, — which is published bi-monthly at Berlin, and is edited by the distinguished Comenius scholar, Dr. Ludwig Keller. This review has most creditably carried out the purposes of the society in publishing a wealth of original material on Comenius and his contemporaries, that hitherto has been altogether inaccessible to the student of the history of education. The society also publishes a bi-monthly educational journal for the use of teachers in the elementary schools of

Germany especially interested in the doctrines of
Comenius. It is entitled *Comenius-Blätter für Völks-
erziehung*, and is also published at Berlin and edited
by Dr. Keller. The propaganda of the Comenius
Society has done much to restore this worthy to the
place he so justly merits — the foremost educational
reformer of modern times.

These are some of the agencies employed by the
Comenius Society in opening up an appreciation of
this great man, who, "born in Moravia, working
amongst Czechs, Germans, English, Dutch, Swedes,
and Hungarians, with friends in France and Italy, has
won by his thought, as well as by his life, a universal
significance. As philosopher and divine, in union
with Andreæ, Dury, Milton, and others, he devoted his
life to a work of peace. He placed the weal of man,
as he termed it, above the respect for languages,
persons, and sects; thus his energies were directed
toward restraining the wrangling people, churches,
and classes from the violent utterance of their differences, and leading them on the ground of early Christian views to mutual peace and forbearance. As
educationalist, inspired by Bacon, he successfully
asserted the claims of experimental science in the
elementary schools of his time, placed the mother-
tongue on the list of subjects of instruction, and
included in the conception of the school the idea of
physical culture. By his demand for education of all
children, including girls, who till then had been
neglected, he became one of the fathers of modern
elementary education."

APPENDICES

I. TABLE OF DATES

(a) *Pertaining to the Life of Comenius*

1592. Born at Nivnitz, Moravia, March 28th.

1604. Death of his father and mother.

——. Entered the elementary school at Strasnitz.

1608. Entered the gymnasium at Prerau.

1611. Matriculated in the college at Herborn.

1613. Matriculated in the university at Heidelberg.

1614. Appointed teacher in the Moravian school at Prerau.

1616. Ordained as a minister, April 29th.

1618. Called to the pastorate of the church at Fulneck; also superintendent of schools.

1624. Marriage to Elizabeth Cyrrill.

——. Driven into the Bohemian mountains by religious persecutions.

1627. Banished from his native country.

1628. Fled to Poland; given charge of the gymnasium at Lissa.

1632. Consecrated as a bishop, October 6th.

1641. Called to England, arriving there September 22d.

1642. Left London, June 10th, for Sweden.

——. Settled at Elbing, Prussia, in October.

1648. Returned to Lissa; death of his wife; chosen president of the council (senior bishop), of the Moravian Church.

1649. Re-married, to Elizabeth Gaiusowa.

1650. Took charge of the schools at Saros-Patak, Hungary, in May.

1654. Returned to Lissa.

1656. Lissa burned; flight to Silesia.

——. Settled in Amsterdam.

1670. Died at Amsterdam, November 15th; buried at Naärden (Holland), November 22d.

(b) *Principal Writings of Comenius*

1616. *Grammaticæ facilioris præcepta* (Simple grammatical rules). Prague.

1617. *Listové do nebe* (Cries of the oppressed poor). Olmütz.

1622. *De Christina perfectione* (On Christian perfection). Prague.

1623. *Labyrint svĕta a ráj srdce, to jest* (Labyrinth of the world and paradise of the heart). Lissa.

1631. *Janua linguarum reserata* (Gate of languages unlocked). Lissa.

1633. *Informatorium der Mutter-Schul* (School of infancy). Lissa.

——. *Atrium linguæ Latinæ* (On the study of Latin style). Lissa.

1634. *Physicæ ad lumen divinum reformatæ synopsis* (Physics remodelled in accordance with divine light). Leipzig.

1638. *Prodromus pansophiæ* (Fragment of the *Great didactic*. Published in London, 1639, by Hartlib). Lissa.

1641. *Via lucis* (The way of light). Amsterdam.

1643. *Pansophiæ diatyphosis, inconographica, et orthographica* (Published in England in 1650 with the title : A pattern of universal knowledge). Danzig.

1647. *Vestibulum Latinæ linguæ rerum* (Vestibule of the Latin language). Lissa.

1648. *Linguarum methodus novissima* (New method of language study). Lissa.

1650. *Lux in tenebris* (Light in darkness — on prophetic visions). Amsterdam.

——. *Scholæ pansophicæ delinætio* (Plan of a pansophic school). Saros-Patak.

1656. *Schola ludus* (School dramas). Saros-Patak.

1657. *Orbis sensualium pictus* (The world illustrated). Nuremberg.

——. *Opera didactica omnia* (Complete didactic works in four volumes). Amsterdam.

1660. *Historia fratrum Bohemorum* (History of the Bohemian brethren). Amsterdam.

——. *Cartesius cum sua naturali philosophia a mechanicis eversus* (Descartes and his natural philosophy overthrown by arguments derived from mechanical principles). Amsterdam.

——. *De natura caloris et frigoris* (On the nature of heat and cold). Amsterdam.

1668. *Unum necessarium* (The one thing needful). Amsterdam.

II. SELECT BIBLIOGRAPHY

(a) *Writings of Comenius*

1. *The great didactic.* Translated with introductions, biographical and historical, by M. W. Keatinge. London: Adam and Charles Black. 1896. pp. 468.

   This first complete translation of Comenius' most philosophic work is admirably done. The biographical introduction is given ninety-eight pages, and the historical introduction fifty pages. These are both interesting and critical. The book unfortunately is not indexed.

2. *The school of infancy: an essay on the education of youth during the first six years.* Edited with an introduction and notes by Will S. Monroe. Boston: D. C. Heath & Co. 1896. London: Isbister & Co. 1897. pp. xvi+99.

   There are numerous foot-notes, intended to show the origin of Comenius' educational ideals and the influence of his writings on later educators. Collateral reading references are given at the end of each chapter, and in the appendix there is a reasonably complete bibliography of Comenius literature.

3. *The orbis pictus.* Translated into English by Charles Hoole. London: John and Benj. Sprint, 1728. Syracuse, N.Y.: C. W. Bardeen. 1887. pp. 100.

   This is a very satisfactory reproduction of the famous Hoole translation by the photographic process. Some of the cuts are indistinct, but Mr. Bardeen wisely refrained from retouching them, preferring occasional indistinctness to modern tampering with the originals.

4. *John Amos Comenius: his life and educational work.* By
   S. S. Laurie. Boston: Willard Small. 1885. pp. 229.

   The introduction (pp. 1–16) gives the effect of the Re-
   naissance on education; a brief but appreciative sketch
   of the life of Comenius follows (pp. 17–64); and the
   remainder of the book is given to an exposition of his
   writings.

5. *Grosse Unterrichtslehre.* Aus dem Lateinischen übersetzt
   mit Einleitungen und Anmerkungen versehen von Julius
   Beeger und Franz Zoubek. Leipzig: Siegismund und
   Volkening. No date. pp. clxxvii+280.

   The sketch of the life of Comenius (176 pp.) is by
   Zoubek, and the translation of the *Great didactic* from
   the Latin into German by Beeger.

6. *Ausgewählte Schriften.* Aus dem Lateinischen übersetzt
   und mit Einleitung und Anmerkungen versehen von
   Julius Beeger und J. Leutbecher. Leipzig: Siegismund
   und Volkening. No date. pp. xvi+359.

   A collection of the miscellaneous educational writings
   of Comenius, including the *School of infancy, Paneger-
   sia*, and fragments of the *Pansophy.*

7. *Grosse Unterrichtslehre.* Mit einer Einleitung: J. Comenius, sein Leben und Wirken. Einleitung, Übersetzung
   und Commentar von Gustav Adolph Lindner. Wien
   und Leipzig: A. Pichler's Witwe und Sohn. 1892. pp.
   lxxxix+311.

   Perhaps the best German edition of the *Great didactic.*
   The biographical sketch is less valuable than the one in
   the edition by Beeger and Zoubek; but the annotations
   on the *Great didactic*, covering about forty pages, give it
   special pedagogic value.

8. *Ueber "Eins ist noth" ("Unum necessarium").* Von
   Joh. Amos Comenius. Znaim: Fournier und Haberler. 1892. pp. 22.

   A convenient edition of Comenius' pathetic swan song,
   "The one thing needful."

(b) *Biographical and Critical*

1. *Educational Review.* Nicholas Murray Butler, editor. New York: Educational Review Publishing Co. March, 1892. Vol. III. pp. 209–236.

    The issue for March, 1892, is a Comenius number. It contains a brief on Comenius by Professor Butler (pp. 209–211) ; " The place of Comenius in the history of education," by Professor Laurie (pp. 211–223) ; " The text-books of Comenius," by Mr. C. W. Bardeen (pp. 223–336) ; and " The permanent influence of Comenius," by Professor Hanus (pp. 226–236).

2. *Proceedings of the National Educational Association for 1892.* pp. 703–728.

    The department of superintendence of the National Educational Association, in connection with the meeting at Brooklyn, February 16–18, 1892, held exercises in commemoration of the three-hundredth anniversary of the birth of Comenius, with the following addresses : " Private life and personal characteristics," Dr. John Max Hark (pp. 703–711) ; " Text-books of Comenius," Superintendent William H. Maxwell (pp. 712–723) ; " Place of Comenius in the history of education," Professor Nicholas Murray Butler (pp. 723–728).

3. *Essays on educational reformers.* By Robert Hebert Quick. New York: D. Appleton & Co., 1893. pp. 119–171.

    One of the best brief critical surveys of the writings of Comenius and written in the fascinating style of the genial Quick.

4. *History of pedagogy.* By Gabriel Compayré. Translated by W. H. Payne. Boston : D. C. Heath & Co. 1886. pp. 122–136.

    A brief summary of Comenius' most important contributions to primary instruction.

5. *The educational ideal : an outline of its growth in modern times.* By James Phinney Munroe. Boston : D. C. Heath & Co. 1895. pp. 68–94.

    A concise and critical survey of the reforms of Comenius

    N

178 APPENDICES

and the other realists. After Quick, the best brief survey
of the modern movement; and at many points it supple-
ments Quick.

6. *Barnard's American Journal of Education.* Published at
Hartford by the editor, Henry Barnard. June, 1858.
Vol. V. pp. 257–298.

Dr. Barnard was one of the earliest to call attention to
the pedagogic value of Comenius' writings. This translation from Karl von Raumer's *Geschichte der Pädagogik*
was, up to the time Professor Laurie's book appeared,
the only comprehensive study of Comenius in English.
Raumer, however, is not an impartial critic of the realists.

The history of the unitas fratrum. By Edmund de Schwei-
nitz. Bethlehem, Penn.: Moravian Publication Office.
1885. pp. 693.

An authoritative account of the Moravian Brethren and
of Comenius' relation to the same.

8. *Monatshefte der Comenius-Gesellschaft.* Ludwig Kellar,
editor. Berlin: Hermann Heyfelder. 1892–1900. 10
volumes.

A high grade bi-monthly review published by the
Comenius Society in the interest of education generally,
and in particular of the views held by the Moravian reformer. The review is a mine of rich material on Comenius and his contempories.

9. *Leben und Schicksale des Johann Amos Comenius.* Von
Anton Vrbka. Znaim: Fournier und Haberler. 1892.
pp. 160.

The best *brief* German life of Comenius. It is accurate
and sympathetic, and contains 17 wood-cuts.

10. *Über des Johann Amos Comenius Leben und Wirksamkeit.*
Von Anton Gindely. Znaim: Fournier und Haberler.
1893. pp. 109.

Another brief German work. Professor Gindely is a
Roman Catholic, and while he writes of Comenius with
less enthusiasm, he presents his life with critical fairness.

11. *Johann Amos Comenius: sein Leben und seine Schriften.*
Von Johann Kvacsala. Berlin: Julius Klinkhardt. 1892.
pp. 480 + 89.

This, so far as I know, is the most comprehensive life of Comenius to be found in any language ; but at many points it is unnecessarily tedious and diffuse.

12. *Rein's Encyclopädisches Handbuch der Pädagogik.* Langensalza: Hermann Beyer und Söhne. Vol. I. pp. 558–569.

An excellent brief article by A. Nebe. An article on the Comenius-Stiftung follows (pp. 569–573).

13. *Der Anschauungsunterricht in der deutschen Schule von Amos Comenius bis zur Gegenwart.* Von Gottlieb Gustav Deussing. Frankenberg: C. C. Rossberg. 1884. pp. 66.

A historical and critical dissertation on the growth of object teaching and nature study.

14. *Die pädagogischen Grundgedanken des Amos Comenius.* Von Hermann Gottsched. Magdeburg: A. und R. Faber. 1879. pp. 64.

A dissertation on Comenius' philosophy of education.

15. *Comenius: ein Systematiker in der Pädagogik.* Von Walter Müller. Dresden: Bleyl und Kaemmer. 1887. pp. 50.

A dissertation on the contributions of Comenius to systematic pedagogy and school systems.

16. *Die Pädagogik des Spaniers Johann Ludwig Vives und sein Einfluss auf Joh. Amos Comenius.* Erlangen: Junge und Sohn. 1890. pp. 69.

Indicates traces of the educational theories of Comenius in the writings of Vives.

17. *Die Didaktik Basedows im Vergleiche zur Didaktik des Comenius.* Von Petru Garbovicianu. Bucharest: Carol Göbl. 1887. pp. 82.

The influence of the *Great didactic* of Comenius on Basedow and his institution is pointed out.

18. *Schmidt's Encyclopädie des gesammten Erziehungs und Unterrichtswesen.* Gotha: Besser. 1876. Vol. I. pp. 941–951.

The article is by G. Baur. It is less comprehensive, although more sympathetic, than the article in Raumer's *Geschichte der Pädagogik.*

19. *Buisson's Dictionnaire de pédagogie et d'instruction primaire.* Paris : Hanchette et Cie. 1887. Vol I. Part I. pp. 421–427.

Three brief but discriminating articles. The first, on the life of Comenius, by C. Progler (pp. 421–423); the second, on the pedagogical writings of Comenius, by Ferdinand Buisson (pp. 423–426) ; the third, on the permanent influences of Comenius, by A. Daguet (pp. 426–427).

INDEX

Alsted, John H., 43.
Andreæ, John Valentine, 35.
Aquaviva, 3.
Aquinas, Thomas, 7.
Aristotle, *Politics*, 2 ; philosophy of, 7.
Arithmetic, 116.
Arts, 99.
Ascham, Roger, on humanism, 12 ; the *Scholemaster*, 13.
Atrium, 65, 129.

Bacon, Francis, dangers of science, 22 ; views on education, 23-28 ; criticisms on English education, 56 ; education according to nature, 148.
Bardeen, C. W., editor of *Orbis pictus*, 175 ; text-book of Comenius, 177.
Barnard, Henry, contributions to the literature of Comenius, 178.
Barnes, Earl, on the reforms of Comenius, 167.
Basedow, Johann Bernhard, educational theories and labors, 149-153.
Bateus, William, the *Janua*, 36, 125.
Baur, G., sketch of Comenius, 179.
Beeger, Julius, relation to the Comenius-Stiftung, 169 ; translation of the writings of Comenius, 176.
Benham, Daniel, translation of *School of infancy*, 110.
Bibliography of Comenius, 177-180.
Blodgett, James H., call of Comenius to Harvard, 81.
Bowen, H. Courthope, relation of Fröbel to Comenius, 159.
Browning, Oscar, on humanism, 1 ; on the study of Latin, 4.
Bruni, Leonardo, an early humanist, 8.
Buisson, Ferdinand, Vives on pauperism, 18 ; the pedagogical writings of Comenius, 180.
Butler, Nicholas Murray, forerunners

of Comenius, 15 ; meaning of infancy, 86 ; permanent influence of Comenius, 165, 177.

Cæsar, *Commentaries*, 2.
Campanella, Thomas, on study of nature, 35.
Comenius, John Amos, forerunners, 15 ; relation to Vives, 16 ; agreement with Bacon, 23 ; influenced by Ratke, 28 ; obligations to Bateus, 36 ; birth at Nivnitz, 38 ; ancestry, 39 ; classical training at Prerau, 40 ; studies at Herborn, 42 ; matriculation at Heidelberg, 44 ; teacher in an elementary school, 44 ; ordination as a minister, 45 ; exile in the Bohemian mountains, 46 ; flight from Bohemia, 47 ; literary connections, 48 ; first call to Sweden, 49 ; call to England, 53 ; English friends, 54 ; failure of English schemes, 55 ; second call to Sweden, 56 ; relations with Lewis de Geer, 57 ; location at Elbing, 60 ; ordination as senior bishop of the Moravian Brethren, 61 ; ecclesiastical ministrations, 62 ; call to Hungary, 63 ; organization of the schools at Saros-Patak, 64 ; return to Poland, 69 ; flight to Amsterdam, 71 ; complete edition of his works, 72 ; death at Amsterdam, 76 ; burial at Naärden, 76 ; marriage and children, 77 ; alleged call to presidency of Harvard College, 78 ; portraits, 81 ; the *Great didactic*, 83-108 ; the *School of infancy*, 109-122 ; the *Janua*, 123-129 ; the *Atrium* and the *Vestibulum*, 129-139 ; the *Orbis pictus*, 130-138 ; *Methodus novissima*, 138-141 ; influence on modern educators, 142 ; on Francke, 143-

181